THE INSANITY PLEA

THE INSANITY PLEA

William J. Winslade, Ph.D., J.D.
and Judith Wilson Ross

CHARLES SCRIBNER'S SONS
New York

Library of Congress Cataloging in Publication Data

Winslade, William J.
The insanity plea.

*1. Insanity—Jurisprudence—United States.
2. Criminal liability—United States. 3. Trials
(Murder)—United States. I. Ross, Judith Wilson.
II. Title.*
KF9242.W56 1983 345.73'04 82–42650
ISBN 0–684–17897–4 347.3054

This book published simultaneously in the United States of America and in Canada—Copyright under the Berne Convention.

1 3 5 7 9 11 13 15 17 19 F/C 20 18 16 14 12 10 8 6 4 2

Printed in the United States of America.

To Samuel M. Thompson
and
Henry B. Veatch

with thanks

ACKNOWLEDGMENTS

Many people contributed to the production of this book and we are grateful for all their help. In particular, we want to acknowledge the generous assistance of Loren Roth, Nick Thiros, Jack Crawford, Patricia Rees, and Franklin Brockway Gowdy, who provided information about some of the cases discussed in the book; the unflagging goodwill with which Joan McDowell typed the many revisions of the manuscript; the always careful editorial assistance of Annasue McCleave; the reliable encouragement of Ed Park over many months of writing; and the spirited, precise, and informative commentaries provided by Marc Seltzer.

Finally, we are especially appreciative of the many hours spent by Joan Lang, reading the manuscript and giving us the benefit of her rigorous criticism. Although we did not always agree with her views, the clarity and independence of her expression was always beneficial to our thinking.

Contents

Preface

The material presented on the seven cases in this book is, for the most part, based upon court transcripts and judicial decisions. We have limited interviews of participants in order to place the reader as nearly as possible in the same position as the juror in order to better understand the forces that play upon jury decisions.

There is always more to a case than the jury hears. Tensions between lawyers and judges and between lawyers and clients, inadmissible or unrevealed evidence about the crime, and legal strategies for presenting a case are not usually reflected in the written record. Although the jury may be sensitive to these unspoken undercurrents, we believe that most jurors at least consciously try to base their decisions on the courtroom testimony itself. Whether they are successful in doing this is another question.

In any case, we have relied upon the judicial record to

reconstruct the story of these trials. Our discussion does not attempt to ferret out the "real" truth of the crime. Rather, we are interested in understanding the jurors' decisions, shaped as they are by the objective testimony, the psychiatrist-experts' opinions, and the structure of the legal system.

THE INSANITY PLEA

Introduction

EACH DAY BRINGS NEW COMPLAINTS ABOUT AMERICA'S CRIMinal justice system: the courts are soft on crime; the police are corrupt or are more interested in spending time on victimless crimes, such as prostitution and recreational drug use, than on "real" crimes with frightened, injured, or dead victims; juries are biased, uneducated, and nonrepresentative; parole boards recklessly release dangerous people whose crimes were so ghastly that the perpetrators ought never see the light of day again; probation is granted too easily for irrelevant reasons. Rich criminals, we hear, can buy high-priced lawyers to get them off without punishment, while the poor are stuck with public defenders or court-appointed counsel who have no investigators, no budgets, and no time to do anything more than present minimal defenses or plead their hapless clients guilty. Trials are postponed forever. Bail is denied to the worthy, granted to the unworthy. There are even charges that jails and prisons are already overcrowded and that no more criminals should be sent to them. The list of complaints against the legislatures, judges, lawyers, police, and court personnel who structure and keep the criminal justice system running is endless. Perhaps the bottom line of all these complaints is that guilty people go free—guilty people who do not have to accept judgment or responsibility for what they have done and are not held accountable for their actions.

Because we have deeply held beliefs about the great importance of personal freedom and individual action, we also feel strongly about the necessity for personal responsibility. Freedom without responsibility leads to chaos and anarchy. If the external system that offers us the greatest protection from social chaos begins to break down, we are in trouble. So we care about how the criminal justice system works. We care a lot. We believe the guilty should be judged and punished or rehabilitated or imprisoned or executed or something. We do not believe that the guilty should go free.

And yet, the guilty sometimes do go free. That is a fact, not an opinion or an irrational charge by a hysterical, crime-fearing populace. There are guilty men and women who go free not because of constitutional rulings that are necessary to protect all of us from unfair persecution and prosecution, not because there is insufficient evidence to bring them to trial, and not because of human failings, as with inadequate prosecutors or incompetent judges. There are people who go free because we are confused and uncertain about how to think about the human mind. These people go free because their lawyers have successfully pursued a plea of not guilty by reason of insanity by hiring psychiatrists to examine the defendant and to testify to his mental incapacities and to the personal weaknesses that suggest he not be held responsible for the crime he is charged with. These defendants can go free because some lawyers and some psychiatrists are willing to manipulate juries and the criminal justice system precisely in those areas where judgment is most difficult: where judgment is based upon imagining what was in a person's mind when he committed an act.

These are not cases in which the defendant is alleged to have committed a crime. Everyone knows he did it. These are cases in which the defendant goes free because psychiatrists and psychologists—presumed to be expert witnesses on the contents and functioning of the human mind—have been asked by lawyers and are permitted by the law to tell us who is responsible and who is not; who is guilty, and who is insane.

We are troubled by the question of how to assign responsibility. We do not hold children responsible for certain acts because we believe that they are not mature enough to make knowing decisions or to control themselves. We look for reasons behind actions and think that if we understand *why* a person has done something, then perhaps that will help us to decide what responsibility is to be borne by him. We have conflicting cultural aphorisms to guide us on these questions. We believe that, in some way, to explain is to understand, and to understand is to forgive. But we also believe that ignorance is no excuse. The fact of the matter is we are often confused about whether we disapprove of specific acts or disapprove of the motives or intentions of the perpetrator. We don't know whether it is the act or the perpetrator that we are judging. Our confusion is eliminated, we believe, if we can resort to that quintessential twentieth-century solution to hard problems: we refer the problem to an expert.

We ask the expert in this area, a psychiatrist, to rescue us from this troublesome area of judging our fellow citizens and their actions. And the psychiatrist has responded to this impossible request. He has obligingly provided us with his own confusion—no different from our own—but he presents it in an appealingly expert way, with special language and special tests to validate his special knowledge. Unfortunately, it takes more than tests and fancy language to create special, expert knowledge.

How have we come to this peculiar state? If we were to poll the nation, perhaps the moral statement that would come closest to receiving unanimous approval is the belief that killing another human being is wrong. One can imagine societies in which such a belief was not only held by most people but was also a genuine basis of life and political action. Such a society would be very different from ours, for it would demand a full-scale commitment to preserving life, in relation to, for example, foreign policy, automobile safety, alcohol and tobacco merchandising, the availability of guns and other weapons, and the provision of adequate social services to discourage violence in the home or on the streets. Our society, it turns out, does not have *that* kind of opposition to killing humans. While we are opposed to some kinds of killing, we accept and even glorify other kinds of killing.

America has, in fact, an ambiguous and ambivalent attitude about killing and about killers. We take some aspects of this ambivalence from our humanity, for people almost everywhere are both frightened by and fascinated with violent crime. But America, in particular, has long been characterized as a violent nation with a passion for the dangerous life, for crime, and for criminals.

Both the opening of the American frontier and the Civil War have given us a large national experience of violence and, in some areas, an acceptance and approval of violence in what we like to think of as "good causes." The frontier may or may not actually have been as violent and lawless as we imagine it. The reality, however, is not as important as the image held in popular culture. The frontier was a world of good guys and bad guys, but if we look carefully, the good guys and the bad guys all did pretty much the same kind of thing. There were hero-killers and villain-killers on the frontier, but they were all killers. The prototypical figure was the gunslinger, the mythological hero of our frontier tradition. He was the high-noon good guy, who came to kill because that's how it had to be. In reality he was manifested by Wyatt Earp and Elliott Ness, but we even glorify the bad guys, such as Frank and Jesse James, Pretty Boy Floyd, Bonnie and Clyde, and John Dillinger. They are the ground-level folk material of our childhood, whether we know them from song or from film. They are the romanticized rebels who robbed and killed, but were reportedly protected by "the people" from the authorities, because their crimes were somehow acceptable. It was, after all, not some hero but "a dirty little coward" who finally shot and "laid Jesse James in his grave." As a nation, therefore, we both accept and dislike violent crime. Our attitude is ambivalent; our judgment is ambiguous.

Our fascination with violent crime and particularly with murders—the way in which these acts capture both our imagination and our disapproval—may be explained, at least in part, by our moral aspirations. The official morality of the United States is "perfection." Despite the constitutional separation of church and state, most of us believe we are God's own and that we are doing God's work, whether it is taking care of the Indian problem in the nineteenth century or the Vietnamese one in the twentieth. Our destiny is always manifest. We aspire to the best and to be the best, and simultaneously believe we are the best.

But it is difficult to hold up the banner of perfection, when we have not in fact yet achieved it, because we must spend some considerable amount of time and energy hiding, denying, and disguising those darker aspects of our personal and national psyche. Criminals are those among us who have not kept those dark impulses hidden. Because our official stance is perfection, we may secretly or unconsciously rejoice at the opportunity to see jealousy, envy, resentment, hatred, or bitterness take away life as they do in violent crime. We do not sanction such feelings in the public version of our national and individual character.

With great sincerity, we bring duty, hope, and a belief in the perfectibility (if not the perfection) of our intentions as the guidelines to our daily lives. But we always understand these qualities in terms of their opposites: committed to duty, we worry about the threat of lawlessness, lack of discipline, laxness, falling standards, and the collapse of morality. Hopeful ourselves, we fear the results of cynicism and bitterness in others. Striving for perfection, we look away from acknowledged failure. We worry about those losses in others more than we fear them in ourselves. But when we recognize what may be murderous qualities in others, we vibrate with them, recognize them as possibilities within us as well. It is safest for us to feel this commonality when the outlaws are conveniently dead and can be safely romanticized. We do not usually do it when the criminal is alive, at large, and unknown, but sometimes our interest is captured by violent crimes and criminals of the present, once the alleged perpetrators are captured and placed on trial.

These murderers intrigue us when we do not have to think much about the reality of their acts; when we are free to roam about in their intentions and to imagine what led them to such actions. We are then free to find some part of ourselves in their story: the anger *we* would have felt had a flirtatious girl been so rejecting; the rage *we* would have had to control if a superior had lied to us and publicly stolen a reward that was rightfully ours; the agony *we* would have endured when a callous spouse flaunted her infidelities and then denied us the right to see our children. We can imagine the rage, anger, hopelessness, and bitterness that such situations call forth in humans. *We* would not act upon those feelings ourselves, of course. We would control them and act within the stern and clear requirements of duty, hope, and the perfectibility of our intentions. But we see that there are others who do not, and perhaps cannot, accept the yoke of those requirements.

In order to experience these empathetic feelings for the criminal and his actions, we must know something of the story behind the crime. When we hear the tale of the criminal, we can imagine how he felt and what led him to the violent act. When we know only the crime itself, our reaction is different, for it is the person, not the act that draws us. We may love, pity, and romanticize Bonnie and Clyde as we imagine the boredom and personal pain that drove them to their acts, but we remain opposed to and do not glorify bankrobbing. The act and the person who performs the act can be very different for us; and we can, with our easy tolerance for ambiguity in these situations, deplore the act and embrace the criminal.

We *are* opposed to crimes of violence. When we hear a radio news bulletin informing us that an elected official has calmly walked into city hall and shot two other elected officials, we are genuinely appalled. When we open the morning newspaper to read of the death of an innocent ghetto youth at the hands of a white policeman, we are sickened. The abused wife who poisons her husband or the deserted husband who attacks his ex-wife and her paramour are examples of crimes that most probably will not evoke our sympathy—because the act of murder is repellant.

But the American judicial system does not try to punish acts. In court, the *person* is placed on trial, and it is the person who interests us. Those of us who learn about the act that was committed usually know only the barest of details, culled from newspaper or TV news stories, and do not know much about the person. Nor are we likely to gain access to the story of the criminal. We are left with abhorrence of the act and the expectations of swift justice for the evildoer.

But when these cases come to trial, the issue of the person is often a substantial part of the case, for the question may be, why did he do it? And to know *why*, we must first ask *who* is this person and what is his nature? The jurors then must hear the defendant's story.

The law assigns psychiatry and psychology a special role in explaining a person to a jury. The observations and knowledge of acquaintances, friends, and relatives are all relevant to the explanation, but the psychiatrist or psychologist has a distinct charge, for he alone is a specialist in deciphering the mind. He alone can talk about whether the defendant could have had the capacity to form intent, could understand the nature of his actions and whether they were right or wrong, and could control his actions if he wanted to. When the jurors have listened to this speculative testimony, they are not asked to judge whether "*this* person did *this* bad act." Instead, they must decide, "Is this person, who admits to having done this bad act, a good person or a bad person?" Did he do it on purpose (a bad person), or did he do it by mistake (a good person)?

The stories of these trials are not like the detective or mystery stories that are an enduring part of our literary heritage. In mystery novels, the question is always "who did it?" In trials where the primary plea of the defendant is not guilty by reason of insanity, we do not have to question who did it; we know the defendant did it. Any number of people may have seen him do it, he himself may have confessed to doing it and there is ample corroborating evidence, or, occasionally, he may have done it on television. Then there is no puzzle, for the presence of the insanity defense makes the question "who did it?" irrelevant. But the insanity plea brings up much more complex and far more puzzling questions: "What was he like when he did it? Was he a person just like you and me? Or was he different from us? And if so, how much different?" Scientific thinking, however educated, is not likely to give us a clear answer to these questions.

"Who did it?" is a question of fact, one that is, at least theoretically, capable of being answered definitively. "What was the perpetrator's state of mind when he did it?" is not a question of fact, for we do not even know what we mean by "state of mind," cannot define its elements, and, even if we could, would have no way of telling whether the definitions were met in a given case. It is theoretically possible to determine—by direct or indirect evidence—whether, for example, a person fired a gun. He could have been seen firing the gun; electronic cameras could have photographed him firing the gun; paraffin tests made on his hands would determine whether there was physical evidence of his having fired a gun within a certain period of time. There may be circumstantial evidence: A man is seen holding a gun, a gunshot is heard, and the man holding the gun runs away. All of this is acceptable evidence and any of it would permit us to make some acceptable, reasonable judgments about whether in fact the man had fired the gun.

A trial that features an insanity defense does not ask that kind of question. Instead it asks "did the man mean to fire the gun and cause the injury?" or "could he or did he *choose* to fire the gun?" None of the factual evidence is relevant here. With an insanity defense the trial asks a question about an internal, subjective phenomenon, about the state of mind, which cannot be observed by others, photographed by cameras, or tested retroactively. While there is no external, direct evidence of a state of mind, even indirect evidence is weak. Suppose the man was smiling when he fired the shot. What can we infer from his smiling? Interpretations could range from his being happy to be shooting the gun (and intending to shoot it) to his thinking that he was watering a plant, believing the gun was a watering can. We know no more about his state of mind from the fact that he was smiling than we would know if we had not been told that he was smiling.

What is a judge or juror to do when asked to answer such a question? In the American legal system, judges and jurors have turned to psychiatrists for a hundred years to receive guidance in answering these questions. The insanity plea, the diminished capacity plea, and the irresistible impulse test all demand the expert testimony of psychiatrists and psychologists, the specialists in the study of human behavior, human thought, and the human mind.

The introduction of psychiatrists as expert witnesses in criminal trials does not, unfortunately, solve the problem of how to discover human motives, intentions, or states of mind. In fact, it brings with it new problems. The first of these is the assumption that psychiatry is based on a scientifically tested theory and body of knowledge and that the elements of this body of knowledge can be defined, assessed, and measured in some way (if only statistically), applied consistently to the issues at question, and used for making predictions in criminal trials. An expert witness is presumed to be in possession of a kind of technical, replicable knowledge that is otherwise unavailable to the jury or to the average person. For example, blood chemistry experts are used because blood stains are not always visually identifiable nor can they be identified as being from a specific person without performing special tests. The expert witness can perform those tests, make conclusions, and provide the specific and at least statistically reliable information on which the jury can rely and which it can obtain in no other way.

Psychiatry does not have the kind of scientific base that exists for such areas as forensic pathology. Much psychiatric theory is still disputed, with great disagreements existing about what kind of behavior is abnormal, whether abnormality is a function of heredity or environment, whether abnormality can be manifested psychologically without a physical, bodily component, and whether diagnoses are anything more than descriptions.

If, for example, the diagnosis "schizoid personality disorder" means nothing more than that a person has delusions that last for short periods of time, psychiatric labeling is of little use, since it only applies an arbitrary, impressive-sounding name to behavior that an ordinary person could observe and describe for himself. If anything, diagnostic labeling may make the behavior seem more serious than ordinary language would. In this instance, psychiatric expertise is not only not helpful but can actually mislead jurors. If jurors are not familiar with the vagueness and imprecision of the underlying assumptions that psychiatrists have about diagnosing mental illness, they may well take psychiatric opinions to be far more precise and scientifically accurate than in fact they are. When a psychiatrist gives his opinion in a court case, it is truly his opinion only. Even when it comes to diagnoses, there is ample research evidence that there will be substantial disagreement in any group of psychiatrists about how to categorize behavior. They may not disagree about certain kinds of diagnoses where the symptomology is very different (for example, clinical depression as opposed to paranoid schizophrenia), but many disorders have overlapping symptoms and there is no clear way to differentiate them from one another. This is especially true of mental disorders with delusional symptoms.

The bulk of psychiatric testimony does not rest on any kind of testing. Rather, it is the psychiatrist's impressions drawn from a series of interviews with the defendant. Because his conclusions rest so fully on information drawn from questioning the defendant about his past, his thoughts and feelings, and events surrounding the acts in question, many critics contend that jurors could just as easily draw their own conclusions about the defendant's state of mind. They argue that the jury has no need for the psychiatrist as an intermediary or interpreter between them and the defendant.

For example, if a psychiatrist says that the defendant, who has admitted to raping and murdering two women, has a schizoid-type personality characterized by occasional disorientations, and was an abused child, is the jury in any better position to judge his actions than if they only knew that the defendant, who was beaten by his mother when a child, had graduated from high school, held a job, lived with other people amicably, attended movies, paid his bills, and raped and murdered two women? The psychiatrist would contend that his diagnosis is valuable, scientific information that is otherwise unavailable to the jury. But does it have any relevance if he can tell the jury nothing about the nature of this defendant's disorientations, nor whether or not the defendant had them at the time of the killing or even ever had them prior to the crime—or in fact ever really had them? All he knows is what the defendant tells him. And the defendant who is planning to make an insanity plea has every reason to tell the psychiatrist whatever he thinks will get him off. It is the defendant alone who has firsthand knowledge of what was in his mind. And if he alters or invents information, who can prove the falsification? Permitting—even encouraging—psychiatrists to make judgments about the defendant's state of mind at the time of a crime based on the defendant's own version of events invites the defendant to present indirectly through the psychiatrist an exculpatory version of what happened. If the defendant (or his attorney) believes such information is relevant or important to the defense, then the defendant is free to take the stand and to provide his view of events—however self-serving or incoherent—and allow the jury to assess it directly.

Psychiatry can contribute to the trial process by giving names to behaviors, but such a contribution does not make the judge's or jury's decision about guilt easier or more accurate. If psychiatric information has any value in this arena, it is solely in respect to decisions about treatment and treatability of a defendant. On that topic, jurors, judges, and lawyers are unlikely to have any specific knowledge, and it is important to know whether a defendant's crime is related to some mental complex that is amenable to treatment. If there is little or no prospect of successful treatment, we should not use mental health treatment expectations as a way of expressing our compassion for, or confusion about, those who have for one reason or another touched a sympathetic vein within us.

The second—and truly insurmountable—problem with bringing psychiatry into the legal system is the fact that the law and psychiatry are philosophically incompatible. The law tells us that if we commit illegal acts, we must be punished. But the law assumes that we have freely chosen to perform these acts. Psychiatry does not make any such assumption about free will or choice. Psychiatric theory is deterministic and assumes that behavior is caused, shaped, or determined by prior events—either immediate events or those in the distant past—or by physiological states. For example, to the psychiatrist, an abused child is likely to become an abusive adult because he has learned from his parents that violent behavior is acceptable. He does not choose to abuse others. Or the psychiatrist may believe that chemical imbalances or chemical deficiencies within the brain will precipitate certain violent behaviors when certain external stimuli are present. In neither case could one be said to be "responsible" for the violent action in the sense that one chose it, for one does not (at least within the ordinary meaning of the word) choose either one's parents or one's brain chemistry.

When the criminal justice system and the psychiatric profession meet in the courtroom to decide about guilt, very different ideas about individual responsibility emerge. This collision often results in an enigmatic and curious product: a jury decision that seems inexplicable given the facts. When juries judge "craziness," they very often produce a crazy kind of justice. In some cases, the jury's attempts to mesh psychiatric testimony and legal definitions seem an exercise in public fraud: confessed murderers can go free, and madmen may be sent to prison.

If we view legal and psychiatric theory about individual responsibility as mutually exclusive claims, it is hard to imagine why anyone ever thought that they could be brought together to function harmoniously in a single system. But history provides ample evidence of the continuous struggle over the past two thousand years to find a way to understand and cope with madness within civilized societies.

The Greeks had an aphorism: Those whom the gods would destroy, they first drive mad. Although Hippocrates developed an elaborate physiological explanation of *how* the gods caused madness, the aphorism suggests that the mad were seen as men who had unwisely attracted the attention of the gods and had been struck down for their lack of discretion. This view of madness gives the madman a kind of importance—he is someone *beyond* ordinary men, not someone *beneath* them. Roman law accepted this view and, in effect, made the insane nonpersons, i.e., beyond the category or the realm of persons. Lifetime guardians were appointed for the mad, and, in all periods during which the individual was insane, the guardian was held legally responsible for his acts.

Christianity altered this view of madness, though it did not always alter how madness was treated legally. The strength of Christianity's view was that it provided a concept of madness that took account of both legal and theological concerns. St. Augustine believed that the insane could not be punished for any illegal act that they committed while insane because they lacked the will to do the act. This sounds very similar to the current jurisprudential view that sees insanity reflected in the inability to intend to commit an illegal act or to understand its wrongness—in effect, an absence of will, of freely choosing the act. In fact, however, this view is not the same as the current one, because the conclusion that St. Augustine (and the medieval period) reached was derived from religious beliefs rather than from medical ones.

Insanity was, to medieval thinkers, a loss of reason that resulted from sin, but it was not itself a sinful state. God, they believed, had many ways to punish sin, and insanity was one of his most severe forms of punishment. This was because it was man's reason that brought him closest to God and to deprive him of that reason left him most separated from God. When separated from God by madness, a man was devoid of will and reason. He could not, of course, be punished for acts performed while mad, but he could be and was punished for those sinful, if not necessarily illegal, acts that had brought the punishment of madness upon him. The final judgment on the acts of a madman was not, as it is in our time, "If he's crazy, let him go." Instead, upon regaining his sanity or becoming lucid he was required to accept punishment or do penance for those sinful acts that had resulted in his insanity. He was, in this way, held accountable for *something*.

In the medieval world, religion and law proceeded from the same assumptions and the same understanding of human nature, and the church and the courts were united. In today's world, law and psychiatry (to many, a secular form of religion) do not share a common view, and as a result, when they operate together, no sense of accountability is found.

Most European countries adopted Roman law and did not hold the mad legally responsible for their actions, but the English did not adopt this view. Instead, English law maintained that one did not need to be in possession of one's full powers of reason to commit crimes or to be found guilty of them. Under English criminal law, the mad could be found guilty and the king could pardon anyone he believed not to be morally guilty because of insanity. In English civil law, the mad were held responsible because intent or motive was not an issue. They were, on the one hand, at least minimally protected by the law—either by pardons or by guardian appointments—but they were generally feared because they alone, as a result of this protection, had the right to act without fear of retribution. This tension continues to exist and plagues our thinking about how to deal with madness in a society where behavior is often controlled only by external standards of legality.

The psychologizing of Western culture began in the mid-nineteenth century, and it is not surprising that insanity defenses became much more common during that period, primarily as a result of the 1843 *M'Naghten Case*. After that case (in which M'Naghten killed the secretary of Prime Minister Sir Robert Peel, thinking his victim was Sir Robert and believing that Peel was persecuting him), criminal guilt could be avoided if a person could prove that, by virtue of a mental defect of reasoning, he did not know what he was doing or did not know that what he was doing was wrong. Although this must have seemed a great and progressive advance in a country that was intensely concerned with social and humanitarian reform, it has not, in the long run, served either Americans or the English well. In permitting such defenses, the legal system attempted to provide a place within it for the new "psychological" and "scientific" view of man, and the humanistic concerns that traveled with psychology. But neither psychiatry nor the law can subsume the other. They are competing, equal, and contradictory systems about how to look at behavior. In spite of that, the law has decided that individual responsibility for behavior is the rule except in certain instances, such as permanent or temporary insanity, diminished capacity, or irresistible impulse. Law is not able through legal expertise, however, to tell when such exceptions occur. Only psychiatric expertise can determine that.

It was the belief that such judgments were in the hands of objective scientists that allowed the law to be even marginally comfortable with this reduction of human responsibility. Psychiatrists, who are medical doctors working within a scientific tradition, could surely be trusted to provide accurate information to the courts. Unfortunately, the theoretical structure and the predictive and explanatory capabilities that psychiatry aspired to did not develop as psychiatrists had expected they would. In practice, psychiatry was no more able than the law to identify or predict temporary insanity, irresistible impulse, or diminished capacity. Only when mental illness became so pronounced, so florid, that even the most casual observer could spot it were psychiatrists able to agree on the meaning of abnormal behavior. As it turns out, psychiatry can describe behavior and offer explanations for it, but it cannot determine the "truth" about the state of mind of a human being either in the present or in the past any better than can the nonexpert using common sense. Because psychiatry aspires to being a science, it often promises greater precision than it can deliver; in practice, it operates as a kind of groping pragmatism.

Psychiatry has an honest disagreement with the law about how to assess and alter human behavior. But it would be far better for everyone if it did its disagreeing outside the legal system rather than within it. When psychiatry battles to affirm its views from inside the criminal justice system, society is left not knowing who is running the show. It is as if a snake (the law) swallowed a small mouse (psychiatry). The mouse, however, refused to be digested and now lives happily inside the snake, growing bigger every day. We are not at all sure whether what we have is a snake who has eaten an indigestible mouse or a mouse who wears a very elaborate skin. As the criminal law system handles many serious crimes of violence, the psychiatric model for responsibility often appears to have far greater authority than the legal model. As the attorney for one mass murderer pointed out, people who commit such horrible crimes as those his client committed cannot be thought of as responsible people, for if they were responsible people, they would not commit such crimes. The crime, he said, speaks for itself as to his client's craziness. Such a view leaves no room at all for the law's views of responsibility.

The underlying theory of American law is that an individual is responsible for his actions and that if he violates the law, he should expect to be found guilty and punished; and that society has the duty to find him guilty and to punish him. The standard for this responsibility is the knowledge of right and wrong and the ability to choose either course. The law asserts that people know—or should know—what is permitted and what is not permitted, that they are free to choose and that they must accept the legal consequences of their choices.

When psychiatrists attempt to explain behavior, they can dilute or even eliminate the idea of personal moral responsibility for past actions. Social psychology often substitutes cultural, social, or familial responsibility—that is, some kind of group responsibility—for individual responsibility. The individual may or may not *learn* to exercise greater control over his behavior, but even this learning will be influenced by the social environment. The idea of group responsibility in its lightest and wittiest form is heard in the song "Officer Krupke," from *West Side Story*, when the juvenile delinquents proclaim "We're depraved on accounta we're deprived."

Therein lies the heart of a real paradox. If you're depraved because you're deprived, what is the use of punishment that will offer you only further deprivation? Are these people depraved because they're deprived or depraved because they choose to be depraved? Are they victims of larger, historical issues, of biological determinism, or are they independent actors? And how could we know?

In the courtroom these questions are almost ritually enacted. The prosecution contends that the accused is a person acting as an independent decision maker; the defense attorney explains that the accused is the victim of forces beyond his control. Since these two views are mutually exclusive and since neither can be empirically proved, the question is placed in the hands and minds of twelve jurors.

When a jury faces such a question, what often becomes a "satisfying" (at least to the jury) conclusion is not careful application of either legal definitions or psychiatric expertise. Rather, given all available information, attitudes, and insights, the jury determines what seems to them at the moment as *fair*—what, in essence, reflects the jury's feeling that their decision provides balance to the competing claims. Or, it may be the result of jurors being persuaded by one or more particularly good psychiatrist-performers.

The jury's position is a very difficult one and may lead to more hung juries than in the past. Whom are they to believe? When the jury decides whether the person before them is a responsible human being, psychiatric views may become too inflated relative to ideas about paying social dues. In that case, the jury may attempt to redress the imbalance with a relatively harsh verdict. If the legal view of responsibility becomes too inflated, then the jury may try to strike a balance by extending greater compassion. Or they may simply give up in the face of the conflicting claims and reach no decision at all.

In the past few years, the insanity defense has been successfully used to free an abused wife who murdered her husband and to free a young man who shot and killed his paraplegic brother at the brother's own request. The insanity defense, diminished capacity defense, and/or extensive psychiatric testimony partially exonerated Dan White, the San Francisco County Supervisor who murdered Mayor George Moscone and fellow supervisor Harvey Milk; freed Prosenjit Poddar, who murdered a nineteen-year-old college student, the unavailable girl of his dreams; freed Leonard Smith, who murdered baseball's best boy, Lyman Bostock; and freed Officer Robert Torsney, who shot to death a fifteen-year-old black ghetto youth who was strolling down the street on Thanksgiving night. Fortunately, it didn't free Tex Watson, the drug-ravaged hippie who led the Manson killers through their murderous spree. The irony is that Tex Watson was probably far crazier at the time of his crime than were any of those freed by psychiatric testimony and insanity defenses.

The not guilty by reason of insanity plea is not used very often and is not very often successful. But when it is successful, the result is frequently such an obvious abuse of the idea of insanity and nonresponsibility that the verdict enrages the public and tarnishes both the legal system and the psychiatric profession. Because both lawyers and psychiatrists have critical roles to play and contributions to make in our continually troubled society, any activity that brings them into disrepute or uses their resources foolishly needs to be seriously questioned, criticized, and revised or eliminated. An elimination of the insanity plea or the removal of psychiatrists as expert witnesses (or even informed speculators) would not bring us a golden age of justice or even significantly reduce crowded court calendars. But it would eliminate some egregious and highly visible offenses to good sense. It would permit psychiatry and psychiatrists to return to their proper concern with treatment of illness and alteration of behavior. It would restore the law to its proper concern with assigning guilt for specific criminal acts. And it would, perhaps, even contribute to an enduring sense of our own commitment to duty, allegiance to hope, and belief in the perfectibility of our intentions.

The cases in this book show the law and psychiatry at their worst, struggling openly to resolve their differences. By analyzing these cases, which are particularly transparent battles between law and psychiatry, we can see how and why the insanity plea defeats justice, discredits psychiatry, and enrages the public.

DAN WHITE

A Fatal Promise

On November 18, 1978, when radio and television began broadcasting news of the events in Jonestown, Guyana, the public was genuinely puzzled. The reports were peculiar—at first, all that was known was that one or several members of some religious group had shot and perhaps killed California Congressman Leo Ryan. Apparently Ryan had gone to Jonestown to investigate personally the allegations that many of his constituents were making against Jim Jones, the leader of the group. There were reports that Jones was, in effect, holding people prisoner in the South American religious commune. When the full nature of the events at Jonestown became known, the public was astonished. In San Francisco, where Jones had placed the Peoples' Temple headquarters, citizens were particularly shocked; first, because many of the victims were from San Francisco and thus there was much personal loss; second, because San Franciscans were hard pressed to believe that such a grisly series of acts had somehow emanated from their beautiful, cosmopolitan city.

As the week wore on, the events in Jonestown continued to dominate the news. There were reports that the Peoples' Temple had a hit list of specific politicians who, in the event of harm coming to Jim Jones, were to be eliminated. Insecurity and anxiety increased among San Franciscans as they waited nervously for further information, and for the return of the bodies from the jungle.

Thanksgiving passed. The covers of *Newsweek* and *Time* both fascinated and assaulted the public mind with full-color photographs of piles of bodies at Jonestown. Of course there were madmen in the world, but they could not, would not, have large and loyal followings who willingly, actively did wrong in the names of their leaders. That was something from Hitler's Germany, and not from the United States. How could they all have committed suicide? It must have been mass insanity, or they must have been forced to drink poison, since there wasn't any good reason, such as terminal illness or a life-shattering failure, staring them in the eye. It could not be explained or understood as a rational act for which the victims could be held morally responsible. Crazed, forced, or tricked; those must be the only choices.

On November 27, only nine days after the first news of Jonestown, people all over the country heard another astonishing news flash, one that in some ways was even more bizarre than the news of Congressman Ryan's death. According to the wire reports, George Moscone, the mayor of San Francisco, and Harvey Milk, a city supervisor and leader of San Francisco's politically active gay community, had been shot and killed in their offices in the San Francisco City Hall.

News of political assassinations always comes hard because the victims are in some sense ourselves. They are there because they speak for us, because they represent us, and an attack upon them is an attack upon ourselves. We feel, intuitively, less safe in the order of our lives when our representatives are attacked. Thus, even though most people outside of San Francisco were unfamiliar with the names of Moscone and Milk, they understood the position of their offices and their relation to individual citizens. For those who were familiar with the two men, it would not be difficult to imagine how they might become the target of an assassination plot. Both were clearly identified liberals who had espoused causes unpopular with some parts of the electorate. Harvey Milk was especially vulnerable for he had made no secret of his homosexuality and had fought hard and vocally to protect gay rights. It was not their generally liberal positions that made them an imaginable target, however. It was that they stood for something, and thus a political assassin could find specific evidence of the "danger" such politicians posed to society.

But it was not a Sirhan Sirhan or a Lee Harvey Oswald at work this time. Nor was it a daffy Sarah Jane Moore or Squeaky Fromm who had finally managed to get a pistol loaded and fired. The man believed to have shot the mayor and the supervisor, according to the news bulletins, was yet another member of the board of supervisors of San Francisco, an ex-policeman, a former fireman, and a respected member of the community—Dan White.

It is difficult enough when loners, foreigners, criminals, or madmen murder our leaders. But with this shattering news we had to accept a world in which our leaders murdered one another. We were not living in a banana republic where authority was transferred at gunpoint and mass executions were casual activity. Surely we were not. But in the space of only nine days, the Jonestown massacre and the two murders at the San Francisco City Hall by a duly elected supervisor of the city exploded into our lives.

All American citizens, but especially those in San Francisco, felt the need to account for these events and to provide some psychological explanation. The efforts to do so brought to the surface deep and complex questions about what it means to be a human being and about the boundaries of human responsibility.

Two years later, when the trial of Dan White was over

and the Jonestown deaths were being interpreted in a historical framework, it became clear how our minds had accommodated these events, how we interpreted them so that if we could not feel safe, we could at least feel comfortable with our view of human nature. At Jonestown, it was thought, most of the people had probably been forced to drink poison. In San Francisco, the murder of two fellow politicians was declared a result of Dan White's mental illness. Here then are our only interpretations (other than evil) of grotesque behavior: coercion and madness. It is perhaps almost impossible for us to believe that human beings—people whom we believe to be like us and like others we know, whose humanity we acknowledge to be common with ours—could do harmful and evil acts willingly and knowingly. We can perhaps imagine it in the abstract, but up close it is only when we are able to see them as different from ourselves—as the public saw Charlie Manson and his family—that we can comfortably hold them personally responsible for doing great wrong. But people like us do not do such things. Dan White's attorney, in his opening statement to the jury, made this point clearly.

"Good people," he asserted, "fine people with fine backgrounds simply don't kill in cold blood. It just doesn't happen, and if it does, obviously some part of them has not been presented." When it seems to have happened, he explained, we are obliged to find what it is that we have missed. If the "good people," the "fine people" are like us, if they are not foreigners, or criminals, or loners, or poor, or black, or young, or fringe members of society, or simply wretched in some way or another, then it turns out that what we have not taken into account is that they are mentally ill. For what else could conceivably account for such aberrant behavior?

The trial of Dan White was remarkable not only because the verdict was so unexpected given the known facts and because public riots followed the announcement of the verdict, but also because the prosecution's and the defense's concept of the crime were so different. It was obviously an important case, and District Attorney Joseph Freitas appeared at the beginning of the trial and was involved conspicuously at various pretrial stages. The deputy district attorney who prosecuted the case, Tom Norman, was an experienced and presumably competent senior member of the office. White was charged with two counts of first-degree murder and the district attorney's office believed that they could obtain a conviction easily on both counts. When the trial was over, they had obtained a conviction for voluntary manslaughter on both counts, the least serious charge possible. Since White had admitted that he had shot both men and that it was not an accident, the defense had, through expert psychiatric testimony, prevented White from being held to more than minimal responsibility. It was an unbelievable result from the district attorney's point of view. The acting mayor was appalled, much of the public—knowing the outline of the events that led to the murders—agreed wholeheartedly that voluntary manslaughter was absurd, and many participated in the riots that rocked San Francisco the night the verdict was rendered.

The defense attorney focused the jury's attention not only on the events that led to the murders but also on Dan White and on evidence that was less concerned with motive, intent, actions, or responsibility than with the reconstruction of a man's life, including his thoughts, hopes, and dreams. The underlying assumption of the reconstruction was that explaining the context of an act implies a justification for the act. Thus, to explain is to understand; and to understand is to forgive. The defense attorney and his series of psychiatrist-witnesses explained Dan White to the jury. The jury, seriously committed to carrying out its work in the best and most responsible way, listened to the explanation. Because what they heard was the expert opinion of witnesses trained to explain matters of the mind and because there were no other experts who persuasively disputed their explanation or offered a better one, the jury was obliged to accept and then to understand Dan White. When they came to render a verdict, their understanding allowed them—perhaps obliged them—to forgive. The citizens of San Francisco who reacted so bitterly to the verdict—not only the gay community, but also many politicians, academicians, professionals, and others—had not heard the explanation because they had not attended the court sessions. They were the quicker to judge, to assign responsibility, and to find guilt. They were not persuaded that when an ordinary person behaves in an unusual way in the context of some emotional drama the drama and the behavior together demonstrate the existence of mental illness and the end of personal responsibility.

Dan White's case was a remarkable one, and it has not been without effect. Doug Schmidt, White's attorney, successfully presented a diminished capacity defense to both murder charges. As a result, White was sentenced to a total of seven years and eight months in prison. It is probable that White will serve as few as five years. He is a model prisoner and is likely to receive early release.

The political result of the verdict and sentence was the introduction of a number of bills in the California state legislature to eliminate diminished capacity as a defense to criminal charges and to eliminate comparable defenses, such as irresistible impulse and temporary insanity. The passage of one of these bills in late 1981 resulted, according to many criminal lawyers, in an even more ambiguous role for forensic psychiatrists in their always interesting but seldom convincing attempts to reconstruct the mental states of people they have never met before.

California voters again attempted to restrict the insanity defense in 1981, when they passed the multifaceted Proposition 8. But that was all later. In 1979, Dan White was prosecuted, under the earlier law.

Dan White was thirty-three years old when he shot George Moscone and Harvey Milk. He had been a lifetime resident of the Bay area, had attended local Catholic schools, had been a San Francisco policeman and fireman. His father, also a San Francisco fireman, had died when Dan was seventeen. Dan was one of nine children and, after his father's death and his mother's remarriage, he became one of seventeen children in a large Irish-Catholic, working-class family. Such a family was unusual because of the number of its children, but beyond that it was a family the jury could imagine. These were hardworking, law-abiding parents doing their best—and their best was very intense—to raise their children to be loyal, hard-working, honest adults. Perhaps, with more education, the children would be financially superior to their parents, but they were unlikely ever to be morally superior to them. These were parents with strong views about right and wrong and little interest in ambivalence and indecision. The children would inherit these views.

Dan White was something of a loner in this family, standing apart from the other children. He had been devoted to his own father but saw little of him, and he deeply regretted the loss. Dan did well in school, was active in sports, and served in Vietnam. He completed his military service successfully, returned to San Francisco, and joined the police department—not an unusual choice for an idealistic young man who admired his authoritarian father and who believed in the need for clear rules that were reliably enforced. That Dan White was idealistic was attested to at the trial by numerous witnesses. He believed in goodness, honesty, fairness, in the American ideal of straightforwardness, and in doing what everyone knows is right. His world view lacked any shades of gray. A native of the West, he lived the code of the West—good guys and bad guys. The good guys were straight and honest and did good; the bad guys, for unknown reasons, but probably just because they were bad guys, did bad.

Two years later, White left the police force, traveled for a while, then resumed work with the department. But his career with the police came to an unexpected end when he was faced with a problem that his code did not easily accommodate. He had, while on duty, observed a group of fellow officers beating a prisoner whom they had handcuffed and who represented no threat at all to them.

To Dan White, the police were good guys and the criminals were bad guys, but in this instance the good guys were not doing right. His commitment to doing what was right was so strong that he chose to report the officers, even though he knew that such reporting was against every unwritten rule of one policeman's commitment to another. As a result of his report, he was ostracized by his fellow officers. He left the force, unable to cope with the isolation that resulted, but he probably left feeling that he had been right in standing up against them, even if he had been personally punished for it.

He again traveled about the country, made a trip to Ireland, and then returned to San Francisco, where he applied to and was accepted by the fire department. As before, he sought employment in a field where he could feel that what he did was necessary and important—in fact, was a vital public service.

During the time he was with the fire department, the system by which members of the San Francisco board of supervisors was elected was altered. Prior to 1977, the supervisors had all been elected at large. Thus, it had not been easy for an unknown, unfunded person without political connections to have any chance at the office. But the 1977 elections were different, with supervisors now to be elected by the individual districts. The results of the change benefited both Dan White and Harvey Milk. Each was elected to a first term that year and each was more representative of the constituents of their respective districts than of the citizenry of San Francisco as a whole. White, as a result of an arduous door-to-door campaign that showcased his charm and his personal appeal, easily won the right to represent the eighth district, a low-to-middle-income, blue-collar, conservative district, a district whose demographic characteristics were very much like a profile of Dan White. Similarly, Harvey Milk easily won election as the supervisor of the district in which the gay community is highly concentrated—a district that, like Milk, was sophisticated, educated, white-collar, liberal, and avowedly homosexual.

White had surprised many by his strong showing in the election. He was a young man with no political experience or political connections. He was not well known in the community as a business leader, as a civic leader, or as any kind of public figure. He was a young man who had grown up and into the values of this community, and when he knocked on hundreds of doors and talked with the residents about his campaign for supervisor, they had perceived his honesty and sincerity and had recognized him as one of their own. When this slightly conservative, blue-collar citizenry voted for Dan White, they were voting for a personable young man who exemplified the finest form of their most cherished values. They entrusted their voice to White and he, as they must have sensed he would, took this trust very seriously. There was no room in Dan White's view of life for the wheeler-dealer, buy-and-sell, compromise-to-improve-your-position politician. He saw himself as a shining presence, working for the good of his people.

It was not long, however, before the victory turned a little sour. A supervisor's position in San Francisco is considered only a part-time job and the pay in 1977 was $9,600 per year. No one expected supervisors to live on that salary, since they were also expected to hold another job. Only Dan White, however, worked for the city in his "other" work, too, and the city attorney's office believed that full-time employment by the city was a conflict of interest for an individual also holding a supervisor's position. White had to choose either his work as a fireman or his newly gained supervisorship.

It was not a ruling aimed at White particularly, because the question had not come up before. It was surely a difficult choice for White, especially since his wife was about to leave her job because of the impending birth of their first child. The decision to keep the supervisor position was made possible when White obtained a loan to buy a fast-food stand, The Hot Potato, on the San Francisco wharf. With a business that he and his wife could operate and that would not interfere with his supervisor duties, White was able to leave the fire department, though doubtless with much regret. He had enjoyed being a fireman and had even been awarded a medal for rescuing a woman and her child. It was work that would have left him with a clear feeling of service and contribution to the welfare of others, but the supervisor's position had an even greater possibility of satisfying this need.

Perhaps it was not fair that White had been required to leave the fire department. Other elected officials had involvements with the city in connection with their businesses, and they simply did not cast votes whenever there might be a conflict of interest. White, similarly, could have exempted himself from any vote that had to do with the fire department or that would benefit him as a fireman. Still, he had left the fire department, and perhaps he would be all right, although the new business required a great deal of his time. His son, born early in 1978, brought him a new sense of family as well as additional demands for his time, and his supervisor's work was equally demanding. There was so much to learn. Suddenly he had three new careers—father, small businessman, and elected official—each important and each needing more of his time than it was possible to give.

A novice in politics has much to learn and, if he is idealistic, much of what he must learn will be very discouraging. Because the rhetoric of politics is steeped in high principles and noble beliefs, many people believe that a politician's daily life and everyday work are similarly composed of high ideals and good works. The discovery that principles frequently fall to personal loyalties or to personal advantage is a harsh lesson for the naive idealist. This discovery is not easy to reconcile with a belief that an action is always either good or bad, that everything counts, that a promise is a promise, that a man's word is as good as his deed, or that fairness is the American way.

White must have taken these political lessons hard. By November 1978 the demands of his business, family, and elected office were becoming too great for him to handle easily. The stress of his life was ever-increasing and he felt that he must do something to create some kind of balance. Something had to give. Suddenly, without discussing the matter with his wife, family, political advisers, staff, or community supporters, White decided to resign his position as supervisor. Disappointed in the way politicians and politics worked, burdened by the demands of his new business, angry that he had been required to give up his job at the fire department, and resentful that his young son was seeing so little of him, White decided all this could be resolved by resigning as a supervisor. His constituents would be better off with someone else.

On November 10, White went into his office, explained to his chief aide, Denise Apcar, that he was resigning, and had her type out a simple letter of resignation. Then he left his office and went down the hall to deliver the letter personally to Mayor George Moscone.

According to the prosecutor in Dan White's trial, this was the beginning of the series of events that led to the murder of Moscone and Milk. The defense attorney, on the other hand, believed that the beginning had come much earlier, when White as a child tried so hard to earn his father's approval and committed himself to a life in which an inner voice always demanded that he live up to the highest standards of conduct and criticized him relentlessly if he fell below those standards for any reason at all.

George Moscone was surprised by White's decision to resign from the board of supervisors. He knew that White had been having financial difficulties, but he had no idea that matters had become as difficult as White's resignation suggested. Although the two men were at opposite ends of the political spectrum, they had always been on good terms. White, outgoing and eager to be liked, brought a convivial presence to the board of supervisors, and Moscone had the easygoing charm of a born politician. As much as they might differ on the issues, they liked one another personally, and Moscone was genuinely sorry that White was leaving. He suggested that White take a few more days to think about it, to see if there were not some way around the problem. White assured him that it was not necessary, that he had thought it through, and that this was the only possible solution. He spoke calmly and confidently, and Moscone finally relented. There was nothing he could do but accept White's decision.

White returned to his office and spoke briefly to the few journalists that his aides had been able to get together on short notice. As in his letter and in conversation with Moscone, White did not have much to say. He was resigning. Family pressures. Financial burdens. Couldn't adequately serve his constituents under the circumstances. He had enjoyed being a supervisor. Hadn't recommended anyone else to Moscone to succeed him. That was about it. One newsman present was an old acquaintance who, from White's point of view, had always been fair in his coverage of White, and when he asked for a personal interview about the resignation, White agreed. But in the interview he had little more to say. After the interview, White left the office, his step lighter with the decision and the burdens of the office behind him.

On November 14, four days later, White again spoke with George Moscone, but this time it was to ask if the resignation could be withdrawn. In the intervening days Denise Apcar and a former aide, Ray Sloan, had been hard at work on White to get him to reconsider his resignation. Both felt they recognized Dan White as a natural politician and a born vote getter. His charm, his fierce honesty and sincerity gave him the kind of charismatic presence that would, they believed, take him a long way. From supervisor, it would be an easy jump to mayor of San Francisco. There was simply no telling how far White could go, but to go anywhere, he had to get his supervisor's job back. In any case, he ought to *want* to get the job back, they pointed out to him, because the district needed him so badly. Certainly no other member of the board understood the needs of the fire and police departments the way Dan did. With Dan on the board, the police and firemen felt for the first time that someone really supported them. They felt let down when they heard about White's decision to leave office. Dan really owed it to all those people to withdraw his resignation.

The suggestion that people were disappointed combined with the vision of a great future in politics could be a powerful persuader for most people, appealing to both guilt and ambition. After a number of conversations, White began to respond to their appeals. Finally, he agreed to see Moscone and to ask him if he could have his job back. White had serious doubts that such a request would be successful, but he was willing to ask.

But Moscone was generous and affable when White met with him on November 14. Of course Dan could withdraw his resignation. Surely a man had a right to change his mind and, if there were any problems with the resignation being withdrawn, Moscone would simply appoint Dan as the new District Eight supervisor to replace the resigning Dan White. White was surprised and pleased by the ease of it all and, when he told Denise Apcar and Ray Sloan, his own excitement was visible. They were convinced that persuading him to take this step had been a good idea. He was the Dan White they remembered—excited, on top of the world, and filled with plans.

On November 15, Dan White and George Moscone each held a press conference. White explained that his family had provided him with enough financial assistance to allow him to devote sufficient time to his supervisor's duties. He was pleased that he would not have to leave his constituents and honored that they felt such regard for him. He had, he said, received many calls from them asking him not to leave, or telling him how unhappy they were about his resignation. Moscone was similarly upbeat at his press conference and said he was glad to have White back as a member of the board.

There was, of course, the practical matter of exactly how to get White's position back for him. Moscone had quickly assigned the city attorney's office the task of finding out whether the resignation could be withdrawn and, if it could not, whether there was any problem with reappointing White to the seat he had just vacated. He didn't expect there to be any major problem and imagined that by Monday, when the board was to hold its next meeting, Dan White would again be one of its official members.

During the next ten days, things moved quickly. What on November 15 had seemed a simple and straightforward problem became by November 26 virtually insurmountable. The original affability of the meetings and press conferences had quickly turned into phone calls to lawyers, terse and formal letters about who said what, and the filing of a lawsuit. The politics of the appointment surfaced and overwhelmed the personal obligation and goodwill that Moscone and White had felt toward one another in their earlier private meetings. Political maneuvering began, something that White had never been able to grasp fully as an activity separate from moral concerns, and it is probable that White believed Harvey Milk was a key figure in those maneuvers. It was on November 15 that White, sitting in the city attorney's office, had overheard a call from Milk. As White understood the conversation, Milk was urging the city attorney to find it legally impossible for White to be reappointed. It was a shocking revelation to White, since he felt that he had always been honest with Milk and had no personal animosity toward him, even though he disagreed with almost everything Milk stood for. It was also the first suggestion that returning to the board might not be as simple as Moscone had said it would be.

On November 16, the day after the press conferences, a group of District Eight residents, the Citizens for Real Representation, announced a rally to oppose White's reappointment to the board. White attended the meeting of disaffected supporters and occasional opponents and, according to news reports, tried to break up the rally. Cameras filmed the shouting between White and the rally speakers. The evening news provided substantial coverage of the meeting and it suggested that the former supervisor was an intemperate man, unloved in his district.

The next day, a rally at City Hall in favor of White's reappointment was organized by his aides. Following that rally, White attended his first meeting with the attorneys who were to provide legal protection for his reappointment. White's aides, as well as other political advisers, had urged him to obtain legal counsel, although White believed Moscone's promise to reappoint him and could not see why he needed lawyers. Finally, he was persuaded at least to talk to the attorneys. The attorneys contacted the city attorney's office, indicating that they were representing Supervisor White in the matter of his retaining his District Eight position. The mayor probably was not pleased to hear this news.

White was making numerous attempts to have his story reach the public and, after leaving his attorney's office, he appeared on a local radio talk show. But while he was speaking confidently about his upcoming reappointment, ten of the Citizens for Real Representation were meeting with George Moscone to explain why they did not want White reappointed as the supervisor for their district.

Moscone was hearing this kind of opposition from more than one quarter. Some of his own aides were opposed to reappointing White because they felt it was not an effective political use of the appointment power. There were also suggestions that other supervisors on the board would welcome a different appointment. Late in the afternoon on November

17, Moscone's secretary located Dan White and asked if he could come in the next day to meet with the mayor. She said the mayor wanted to see White alone and he agreed to be there at noon.

On November 18 another anti-White rally was organized by the Citizens for Real Representation, but White had to miss this one because he was hearing the bad news from Mayor Moscone. Moscone explained that there was political opposition to reappointing White and thus it wouldn't be as easy as he had expected. He didn't say it could not or would not be done, but he did urge White to produce some visible signs of district support, such as letters sent directly to the mayor's office.

A man more politically astute than Dan White would have noticed that Moscone's support was slipping away, and perhaps disappearing, but White did not ask many questions and merely prepared to do what he was asked. Letters could be arranged, because he knew he had support in the district. Throughout the afternoon, as he and Denise Apcar addressed and stamped envelopes for distribution throughout the district, they considered the possible interpretations of the mayor's request. They also listened to the first reports of the murder of Leo Ryan in Guyana. White was shocked by the news.

On Monday, November 20, George Moscone received a memo from Harvey Milk about the gay community's attitudes toward potential appointees to White's seat. None of those mentioned was Dan White. That same day, the board was to hold its regular meeting, but White was not to attend. Instead, on his attorney's advice, he sent a letter to the mayor, with a copy to the board, explaining his reasons for resigning, his reasons for wishing to withdraw his resignation, his understanding of the mayor's verbal promises to reappoint him, and his willingness to not attend board meetings until the legal questions were resolved. Moscone replied the same day in a formal letter, which reiterated the point made to Dan at their recent meeting that there was opposition to Dan in the district, not only from his regular opponents, but from former supporters. Moscone also stated that he planned to take an additional week to consider the matter and, particularly, to better understand the wishes of the Eighth District. He added that he had made no promise to White to reappoint him.

The newspapers immediately got wind of Moscone's change of heart and printed stories about it the next morning, along with reports of the city attorney's opinion that the White resignation could not be legally withdrawn. The city attorney had also concluded that Moscone could appoint anyone, including White, to the vacancy. White was pleased with the city attorney's report, but confused by Moscone's letter and the release of information to the news media.

Unattributed statements began to drift down from the mayor's office to newsmen and City Hall insiders that nobody really wanted White but White. His constituents and other supervisors were all opposed. What could the mayor do? He liked White personally, but if he had no support, it really wouldn't be right to reappoint him. It was the kind of thinking that White himself would be the first to agree with, if it were true, but he knew it wasn't true. He did have support, and with enough letters it could be demonstrated to Moscone. The mayor had just been talking to the wrong people.

When White's attorney and aides saw that Moscone's attitude was changing radically, they began to formulate a legal strategy to keep Moscone from appointing anyone else to the vacancy. White was still reluctant to suggest legal action because he believed that Moscone would do what he had promised. Finally, however, he agreed to sign a letter that outlined a technical objection to the city attorney's opinion that he had officially resigned and could not now withdraw the resignation. But he would not authorize any court action.

On Thanksgiving Day, November 23, one newspaper carried reports that Moscone would appoint a women's activist to the position, while another paper reported that very few letters of support for White had been received at the mayor's office, and that, in fact, the mayor had received more support for other candidates than he had for White. On the strength of these reports, Apcar and Sloan finally convinced White that he should go ahead with a lawsuit, requesting a temporary restraining order to be issued to keep Moscone from appointing anyone until the resignation issue was resolved. The request for the temporary injunction was made in court the next day, but the judge denied it, ordering a full hearing in one week on the matter of whether White's resignation had in fact been properly made. The judge suggested to the city attorney that Moscone not appoint anyone else to the office until after the hearing. The city attorney volunteered to carry the message to the mayor, but pointed out that he did not run the city and could not guarantee what the mayor would do.

There seemed to be little more that could be done by White's supporters. On Saturday, November 25, Apcar organized a petition drive and a Monday morning rally to demonstrate support for White. On Sunday she and four other supporters collected over 1,000 signatures. White did not seem particularly enthusiastic about her achievement when she told him of it, but their conversation was interrupted by a phone call from Barbara Taylor, a local radio reporter. She informed White that she had information from an unnamed source high in the mayor's office that White was not going to be appointed to the supervisor's position on Monday, and, in fact, Moscone was going to appoint someone else. Did he, she wanted to know, have any comment? White knew nothing about it and tried to get off the phone. She pursued him with additional questions. Had he heard from the mayor? Had he received a telegram? Would he pursue his lawsuit? What were his plans? Did he have any thoughts on who might be appointed? White had no comment. Surely Moscone would not appoint someone else without having the decency to call White and tell him what was happening? He hung up and then told Apcar what Taylor had said. It was hard to believe the newscaster could be telling the truth.

The call from Barbara Taylor ran back and forth through White's mind. Moscone had promised that there would be no problem in White's withdrawing his resignation, and if there was, none in Moscone's reappointing him. And now, scarcely a week later, he was appointing someone else. White could not grasp that such a betrayal was possible, that a man of George Moscone's position and reputation would go back on his word, would lie, and would never even bother to explain why he was going to do it or even that he was going to do it. White imagined talking to the mayor, demanding that Moscone be honest with him. Of course, it was possible that Taylor was wrong, that Moscone hadn't decided to appoint someone else, and was still waiting for the proof that White's constituents were behind him. Apcar had assured him that proof of support was not a problem because there were letters, lots of them, and signed petitions. What more proof could Moscone need? Taylor had always been tough on White; maybe she didn't really know anything and was just pushing for a story. It was possible that Moscone was being straight with him.

White slept little that night if at all, going over the events of the past week again and again. In the morning, his wife left the house early. Apcar called from the office to see if he was coming in. A number of his constituents had arrived to demonstrate their support for him, to show Moscone that White was their man, and others would be arriving. Although the news media had not yet shown up, she expected they would be there soon. Moscone was in his office and she thought he probably had seen the supporters gathered in front of City Hall when he drove in. Apcar had seen Moscone talking with Harvey Milk that morning and Milk had seemed to be happy. White halfway listened to Apcar. Perhaps Taylor was right and Moscone was going to replace him with someone more amenable to Harvey Milk's views. White knew Milk had been lobbying Moscone to appoint someone who would be more supportive of the liberal programs that both Moscone and Milk favored. Milk probably still remembered that White had been the only one to vote against the measure forbidding discrimination in housing against gays. But he should understand that White's constituents felt strongly about this issue. Many of them, like White, were Roman Catholics who had very clear views on this issue. It wasn't that Dan was personally against homosexuals, nor did he think that Milk or any other person should be discriminated against. He had always gotten along well with Milk, had even stood up for him on occasion. It was just that White was there on the board of supervisors to speak for his district and for their values. To have voted any other way would have been to betray those constituents. They would not have understood such a vote. Beyond that, White felt that imposing laws that violated people's strongly held beliefs was a bad way to achieve change. It just created more problems, more anger, and more resistance.

White talked to Apcar again on the phone and decided not to go to City Hall. He did not need to make an appearance, for it would not change anything. Then, as soon as he hung up the phone, he began to think about confronting Moscone, about forcing him to admit to White's face that he had gone back on his word. If Moscone planned to push him around this way, then he should have to do it in person. There was no need for Dan White to hide in his house while the mayor told the press that Dan White wasn't good enough to be a supervisor and that White's district didn't want him. It wasn't true, even if Moscone said it was or even just implied it.

White called Apcar and asked her to pick him up at his house right away. He showered, shaved, dressed, and loaded the .38 Smith and Wesson revolver that he had owned since his police days. He took ten extra bullets from the ammunition box, wrapped them in a handkerchief, and put them in his pocket. In the five years since he had left the force, he had occasionally carried the gun, though he had no permit for carrying a concealed weapon. Since he had been elected to the board of supervisors there had been threats against him, and he felt more comfortable with the holstered weapon under his jacket.

Apcar arrived and they made the trip downtown pretty much in silence. As they drove, Apcar tried unsuccessfully to engage White in conversation, to talk about the supporters who had showed up that morning and about the legal actions that were still possible to prevent anyone but White from being seated at the supervisors' meeting that afternoon. White was unusually quiet.

When they arrived at City Hall, White got out of the car, leaving Apcar to park it. She drove on, stopping first to get gas because the tank was almost empty and White had said he wanted to use the car after he met with the mayor in order to meet his wife and tell her what Moscone had to say. He started up to the front entrance of City Hall but, short of the doorway, turned back. He had suddenly remembered that there was a metal detector at that door and had seen that the policeman on duty was not an officer he knew. The gun he was carrying was certain to be detected. White detoured to the side door that was normally kept locked, but for which all the supervisors had keys. Apcar had his and she was sure to come that way after parking the car. White paced back and forth, waiting, but when she did not arrive, he jumped down through an open basement window that was frequently used as an entryway. A man working in the next room heard the sound of White jumping to the floor and came out, asking White who he was and what he was doing. White identified himself and hurriedly explained that his aide had his key to the side door. He continued on to the first floor and the mayor's office.

White went directly to the desk of the mayor's appointments secretary, Cyr Copertini, and asked her if it was possible to see Moscone for a few minutes. Copertini knew that White's appearance in the office just before the press conference at which Moscone would name White's successor was unfortunate. But there wasn't much that could be done about it. She noted that it was 10:00 A.M. She went into the mayor's office and asked him if he would see White. Moscone was not pleased. There was no way that such a meeting could be pleasant for either of them, but since White had come, it was probably right to see him. Copertini asked if the mayor wanted someone else to sit in on the meeting. Moscone decided it was better to talk to White alone. This was, after all, a somewhat sensitive matter, although he hoped that White would not take it personally. Moscone told his secretary to keep White outside for a few minutes, and when he was ready, he would ring her. She left, told White that Moscone would see him in a few minutes, and waited for the call. When it came, Copertini showed White into Moscone's office and returned to her desk. After a while, the sound of raised voices could be heard from the mayor's office, but then Moscone came to the door, looked out, and acknowledged the presence of one of his aides. He winked at him, as if to say that everything was just fine, and shut the door again.

There is no real way of knowing what Moscone said to White or what White said to Moscone. The mayor must have offered White a drink in the inner office, then poured one for each of them, sometime around 10:30. Later in the meeting, they must have talked about Moscone's intention to appoint Don Horanzy to White's post, and about what White would do next. White must have asked Moscone why he had told him he would reappoint him and then backed down, and why he had lied about White's not having any support in his district.

They must have talked about these matters until Dan White drew the gun from his holster and fired four shots. The first two were fired from a relatively short distance and struck Moscone in the chest. The second two were fired from as close as six to twelve inches and went directly into George Moscone's head. Either of the last two shots would have killed the mayor instantly.

Moscone's body lay on the floor as White left the room by way of a back door. He walked quickly down the hallway that led to his own office cubicle and, on the way, acknowledged greetings from several people. An aide of Dianne Feinstein, the supervisor who would become mayor as a result of Moscone's death, spoke to him, telling him that Feinstein wanted to speak with him. White said that he would come by in a minute, that he had to do something first. Feinstein saw White go by, called out to him, but he apparently did not hear her as he hurried down the hall. The clerk of the board of supervisors stepped out of his office and saw White walk quickly down the hallway and turn into his office.

White came back out of his office after a moment and walked across the hall to the cubicle that belonged to Harvey Milk. "Harvey," he said, "can I see you a minute in my office?" Milk assented, got up, and walked across the hall with White. They entered White's office and the door closed behind them.

Not much could have been said, for little time elapsed before Harvey Milk was dead. This time, White shot five times. As before, the first shots (this time three of them) were to the torso. The last two, fired after Milk had fallen, were to the brain. Like George Moscone, Harvey Milk died instantly.

White immediately ran from his office and down the hallway to his aide's office where he grabbed the car keys she had left for him. In moments, he was out of City Hall and driving away. But within an hour, he had turned himself into the police and made a statement, confessing that he had shot both men.

These are the basic known facts of the murders of George Moscone and Harvey Milk. In White's statement to the police, he said he reloaded the revolver in his office before he asked Milk to come in. White's attorney argued that he reloaded automatically, in keeping with his police training. During the trial, White never took the stand. The jury's verdict implies their belief that it was done automatically, as the defense attorney argued, and thus did not suggest any intention to shoot Milk.

During Dan White's trial all this information was brought before the jury. They listened to the tape of White's confession/statement, made shortly after he turned himself into the police. This tape had a great effect on the jury as it was clearly the voice of a man in a great emotional crisis. Still, there was clear testimony that White had been conducting his life in a competent way during the days between his resignation and the deaths of Moscone and Milk. There was ample evidence of anger toward the two men. Bringing the gun and extra bullets with him when he went to City Hall that morning, evading the metal detector at the front entrance of City Hall, reloading the revolver after shooting Moscone and before speaking with Milk, all pointed directly to White's intention and his willingness to commit murder. If this was not an instance of first-degree murder, then what would be?

The jury found White guilty of voluntary manslaughter, not of either first- or second-degree murder. Was it *not* first-degree murder because White had no long-term, carefully drawn plan to kill the two men? Or because he was so angry about the events that had occurred during the week? Would it have been first-degree murder if White had been calm and dispassionate—like a hired killer—both before and after he fired the repeated shots? Would it have been first-degree murder if five psychotherapists had not said they thought White was out of control, depressed, and mentally ill?

Why is it that Dan White was not convicted of first-degree murder? Surely there was adequate evidence to support such a verdict. He was not convicted of a more serious charge because, intertwined with that evidence and sometimes permeating it entirely, was the testimony of the five therapists—four psychiatrists and one psychologist—who had interviewed White at great length and who, each in his own way, concluded that White had a mental illness, was under great stress, and was not responsible for his actions on November 27, 1978.

Each of the experts was asked a series of questions about White's ability to premeditate, to deliberate, and to harbor malice at the time of the murders. These questions were vital because they describe the states of mind necessary to sustain a conviction for either first- or second-degree murder in California. Yet, since none of the experts had seen White until long after the murders, their answers were highly speculative. In addition, these are legal categories, not psychiatric ones, and the law has attempted to ascribe very complex and subtle meanings to each in a fruitless attempt to make the categories more scientific. But they are not scientific, and psychiatrists, when they make such judgments, are not scientists. Each of the five was experienced in forensic psychiatry or psychology, and their understanding of the meaning of the terms was probably as good as that of the attorneys or judges—but that may not be a very high degree of understanding.

Essentially the question they were being asked was:

> (1) Given what you know about Dan White as a result of what he has told you and what others have told you about him, and (2) given what you know as a specialist in matters of the workings of the human mind, about human behavior, thoughts, feelings, and actions, do you believe that Dan White was able to premeditate, deliberate and/or harbor malice on the morning of November 27?

The question was not whether Dan White in fact *did* premeditate, deliberate, or harbor malice, but whether he could have. Surely he could have. Given that the man was acting normally—seeing people, talking, making radio appearances, filing law suits—surely it was *possible* that his mind could premeditate, deliberate, or harbor malice.

Yet each of the five psychotherapists concluded that White did not have those capacities—not even *probably* did not, but definitely did not. He did not have them because, in effect, he lost control. In that sense, the shootings themselves are the proof of White's mental state. If you murder someone and you are not ordinarily a killer, and it is not self-defense, then you have lost control. If you have lost control, then you do not have sufficient capacity to premeditate, to deliberate, or to harbor malice. If you have none of those capacities, then you cannot be found guilty of either first- or second-degree murder. It is a simple and logical progression, each term defining the next, and all depending upon whether you are usually a good citizen.

Three of the psychotherapist-witnesses spoke succinctly on this topic.

> DR. JERRY JONES: Well, I felt that Dan had the capacity to intend to kill. That doesn't take too much to intend to kill somebody. I think he had the capacity also to do something for a base, antisocial purpose and, additionally, I think he had the capacity to know that there was a duty imposed on him not to kill people. But I don't think he had the capacity to hold that duty in his mind while he was acting, so I think that the depression plus the moment and the tremendous emotion at that moment with the depression reduced his capacity for conforming conduct.
> ATTORNEY: In other words, it reduced his control?
> DR. JONES: Yes.

> DR. DONALD LUNDE: In Mr. White's case, he not only did not premeditate or deliberate these killings, but as a result of his mental condition, he was not capable of any kind of mature, meaningful reflection on the morning of November 27th of last year. His mental condition was such that even if he had tried, which he didn't, he would not have been capable of sitting down and maturely, meaningfully, reflecting upon the act, weighing the pros

and cons of doing it, not doing it, doing it in a certain way versus another way, thinking about the possible consequences to the victims themselves, emotional consequences, political consequences, the penalties that might be involved, that sort of thing, all of which is a part of premeditation and deliberation which is necessary for someone to have committed a first-degree murder. None of these things were present in Mr. White at the time or preceding these killings.

DR. RICHARD DELMAN: I think that on the day of the crimes he really had no meaningful, rational capacity to carefully weigh the considerations for and against and rationally decide on a course of action. He couldn't think carefully about what he was going to do. He couldn't appreciate his duty not to do what was wrong and to control his behavior.

The mental illness that the psychiatrists believed White to be suffering from was variously described as "unipolar depressive reaction," "manic-depressive illness, depressive type," "episodes of depression," and "depression of a fairly severe degree." The depression was diagnosed from periods of sleeplessness, weight gain, loss of appetite, and reduced sexual drive. Dan White had periodically had these "symptoms" throughout his entire adult life. His family was accustomed to his "moods," as, presumably, was White himself. He had never sought any kind of treatment, suggesting he had never considered his moods to be a form of illness. Had he done so, the psychiatrists would probably have offered him some kind of treatment for these episodes of depression and he might indeed have felt better. But it is hard to believe that sleeplessness, weight gain, appetite changes, and reduced sexual interest, in combination with the ordinary stresses of ordinary life, justify in any degree whatsoever the murder of two men. It is hard to believe that five well-known, prestigious psychotherapists thought this. Yet, Dr. Martin Blinder testified as follows:

> [The question is] whether or not the anger reaches a degree sufficient to cause a man to lose control. . . . If a man is out of control, then the quality of his premeditation and everything else requiring rational thought is so impaired *as to fall below the threshold of his responsibility* [authors' italics]. In my judgment, the feelings that were seething through this man at the time, anger included—feelings of lack of support, feelings that he had no place to go and that he had no options, that he was letting everyone down—all these things came to a head. These things he'd probably been wrestling with for months. He probably lost control and once a man loses control, I don't know how you can talk in terms of premeditation.

Throughout the psychiatric testimony there was the sense that the doctors believed that only when someone is calmly and carefully thinking can he be held responsible for his actions. When there are feelings involved, and especially strong *negative* feelings of anger or hatred, mere humans are absolutely at the mercy of those feelings. We would all agree that White did not choose his feelings, but the psychiatrists seem to believe that he also did not choose his actions because, if he had chosen them, he would have chosen actions that were more socially acceptable and more responsible. It was not, apparently, Dan White who did these things but some incredible emotional force working within him.

More than three years have passed since Dan White was found guilty on two counts of voluntary manslaughter in the deaths of George Moscone and Harvey Milk. The California legislature has memorialized the event by eliminating the diminished capacity defense, or at least has attempted to do so. The bill was revised a number of times before it was passed, but the conclusion of some lawyers and psychiatrists is that the situation in California is now worse than it was when

Dan White was tried. Presumably, that was not the legislature's intention. As a result of the bill, psychiatrists may no longer testify as to whether or not they believe that a defendant did have the requisite states of mind and whether he did deliberate or premeditate. They may testify only whether he had the *capacity* to deliberate, premeditate, et cetera. Their testimony on the relatively obscure questions has been eliminated. They may now testify only on the totally mystifying questions.

The city of San Francisco has memorialized the event by engaging in a particularly sorry dispute over whether a bust of George Moscone is in poor taste and thus cannot be publicly displayed on government property. The "poor taste" is demonstrated by the fact that the sculpture's base draws explicit attention to this society's acceptance of violent solutions to problems, including the murder of Moscone. Most of those who remember the murders and the result of the trial recall that White got off on the famous (or infamous) Twinkie defense. The newspapers left the erroneous impression that such was the claim of the defense: that is, that White murdered the two men because his brain was addled by junk food. That claim was actually not made at the trial. The defense lawyer argued that a sudden change in White's eating habits, including the consumption of an unusual quantity of junk food, was a demonstrable symptom of White's mental illness. Perhaps the Twinkie defense caught the media's attention and stayed in the public's mind because it seemed as crazy as the verdict.

Despite the wealth of evidence in this case, the jury seemed to have difficulty finding Dan White guilty of anything. We can only speculate as to what made a guilty verdict so hard for them. Did they like White and identify with him? Did they identify with his struggles to make a contribution to the world, only to be betrayed by cynical politicians? Did they fail to identify with the victims simply because they were politicians, and, in the case of Harvey Milk, because he was so open about his homosexuality? Was it a poor prosecution resulting from overconfidence? Did the psychiatrists—certainly quantitatively superior for the defense—present so compelling an analysis of events that the jury was forced to accept psychiatric conclusions against their own common-sense judgment about White's responsibility?

All of these factors are likely to have had some effect, but what seems most likely to explain the jury's surprising verdict is that they found Dan White an extremely sympathetic figure, and not the least because he was so extraordinarily American in his simplistic views of what the world was like. When the jurors thought about Dan White's life and hard times, the ideals of duty, hope, and perfectibility must have lit up in their minds. When his impressive array of psychiatrist-sages came forth with their reasoned explanation for these bizarre, atypical, and entirely inappropriate murders, the jury must have been extremely grateful. They did not need to place the exoneration of Dan White on their own consciences. The medical profession had spoken and they could surely be believed *this* time. Because the defense psychiatrists' views were so amenable to the jurors' willingness to be easy on White, the responsibility for the decision could be divided, masked, and, finally, lost. It is impossible to believe that twelve ordinary jurors would have refused to find White guilty of either first- or second-degree murder if they had not had the psychiatric "scientific" explanation to fall back on. Unfortunately, the "scientific" explanation didn't explain much, nor did it have much substance.

States of mind are continuums, not discrete locations. Dan White had much to be angry about, frustrated about, and resentful of in this uniquely stressful situation, and he failed to control all these very powerful negative feelings. He was depressed and had much to be depressed about, but he was not so depressed that he could not remember to take ten extra bullets with him. If he had drunk himself into a stupor, then driven his car into a group of children, there would be no thought of an insanity plea on the grounds that he had good reason to get drunk and that the alcohol had rendered him unable to know what he was doing. Whether we drive cars or carry guns or both, we must be responsible for the results of our actions.

At the very least, White should have been found legally guilty of homicide. Although he did go to prison, the diminished capacity defense and voluntary manslaughter verdict reduced the sense of legal guilt and mitigated the degree of punishment. Dan White's state of mind could have been a mitigating factor when it came to deciding the form of punishment or the usefulness of treatment. But it had no place in the assessment of guilt itself.

In this instance the criminal justice system became so caught up in what went on in Dan White's mind that it seemed to forget that, as a result of White's actions, nothing went on anymore in Moscone's mind or in Milk's mind. It is true, of course, that a harsher punishment of White or the imposition of a higher degree of guilt would not have altered the events of the past, but that is not the purpose of criminal trials. In part, trials are symbolic rituals to remind us of the standards we try to hold and by which we judge ourselves and others. The psychiatric testimony in Dan White's trial led to a standard of justice well within our reach—and far below our aspirations.

PROSENJIT PODDAR

A Kiss of Death

On occasion, the legal system uses its considerable discretion to balance the competing claims of laws and psychiatry about personal responsibility. Sometimes this is a remarkable balancing act, almost defying logical analysis or verbal description. The California Supreme Court in *Poddar* v. *the People of California* and the companion civil case *Tarasoff* v. *Regents of the University of California* gave such a performance, complete with mid-course reverse somersaults. The problems of the insanity defense are usually manifested in the courtroom. But in both *Poddar* and *Tarasoff*, it was the judiciary that demonstrated why psychiatric testimony and insanity defenses do not belong in a trial determining guilt or innocence.

The basic facts of this case were simple. On October 27, 1969, Prosenjit Poddar, a twenty-five-year-old Bengalese Indian student at the University of California, Berkeley, murdered Tanya Tarasoff, a nineteen-year-old college student with whom he was in love. Her death, the result of a misconceived, misbegotten love affair, should have been no surprise, for it was forewarned by Poddar, by his friend Farrokhg Mistree, and by Poddar's psychotherapist.

Why Prosenjit Poddar should kill the young woman he "loved" but barely knew is a puzzling question. Some clues may be found in discovering how Poddar happened to arrive in America. Poddar had risen with amazing success through the Indian educational system. In the 1960s, he was one of the small number of Indian students chosen because of his intellectual promise to pursue graduate study in the United States in the fields of electronics and naval architecture. Poddar's achievement was all the more impressive when one considers his impoverished background and the prejudices he had been obliged to overcome. He grew up in a tiny village in a remote rural area of India, one of many children in a family of no social consequence. His upbringing was so distant from that of Western society that when he first attended the university in India, his friend Farrokhg Mistree had to teach him how to eat with a knife, fork, and spoon and had to explain plates to him. He was a member of the lowest caste in India, the so-called untouchables. Although the Indian government had legally forbidden discrimination because of caste status, law alone cannot alter custom. Questions of caste still permeated all social decisions in the India in which Poddar grew up. For a young man of such dubious and almost primitive background to have earned the opportunity to be educated in America is clear evidence of Prosenjit Poddar's remarkable abilities, diligence, and desire to better himself.

Many thought Poddar was a genius who was totally devoted to and disciplined by his studies. His arrival at Berkeley in September 1967 was the final stage of preparation for what was expected to be a brilliant career. During his first year, Poddar attended classes and worked at the Richmond Field Station as a naval architect. He applied himself assiduously in his customary manner and met with his customary success. He lived quietly with many other foreign students at Berkeley's

International House (I-House), and in the small periods of time he allowed himself to be away from his work, he tried out some American student pleasures. An occasional drink (liquor had been too expensive in India); brief acquaintances with other graduate students, including women (the undergraduate college in India had been all male); drop-in visits to the weekly folk dancing sessions at I-House were all new vistas from his narrow world of work and study.

A friend from undergraduate days in India arrived to study at Berkeley and Poddar was able to show him around, to help him become acquainted with life in this amazing country. But his friend, Farrokhg Mistree, adapted much more quickly to America. In no time, Mistree was proferring advice to Poddar, correcting his American pronunciation, and making judicious interpretations about the right way to interpret American customs. Mistree had an earlier advantage over Poddar, however, for he had been raised in a large Indian city among a much more sophisticated group of people. For Poddar, familiarity was found in long hours of solitary study.

Then, in the fall of 1968, his second year at Berkeley, Poddar met Tanya Tarasoff at an International Students' Organization folk dance. She talked with him, danced with him, flirted with him. He began to attend the dances more regularly so that he could spend more time in her sparkling company. Tanya told him something of her background, and he doubtless felt some union between them for they were both strangers in this country. Tanya's parents were from Russia, but she herself had been born in Shanghai. Her family then moved to Brazil, and when she was approaching adolescence, they came to the United States. Tanya's background had given her a flair for languages. She was studying them seriously at Merrit College and liked to come to the I-House where Poddar lived to practice conversing.

Tanya was outgoing and friendly with many of the foreign students who lived at the I-House. But as fall passed, Poddar felt that her interest in him was stronger and more special than it was in the others with whom she danced and joked and talked. His interest in her increased, and he began to tell Mistree of the powerful attraction he felt to Tanya.

The attraction brought with it a whole new series of problems. Poddar had never before had any involvement, even of the most innocuous kind, with a woman—either in India or in the United States. He was unsure of how to approach the young woman and, when he did manage to speak with her, he was uncertain of how to interpret what she said and did. That she danced with him, came to his room to talk, and called him on the phone all seemed to confirm Poddar's belief that she cared specially about him, and yet, she spoke of other men, danced with other men, and doubtless called other men. Because he could not understand her actions, Poddar frequently sought the advice of Mistree. Mistree had quickly become more perceptive about American relationships between men and women, and he counseled Poddar sympathetically, but explained to him that although Tanya's friendliness was genuine, it was probably casual and that Poddar ought not to give it too much thought. Indeed, he would do well not to forget that his goal in the United States was to do well in his education—not to pursue romance.

Poddar listened seriously to Mistree's advice, attended to his studies, and tried not to think about the bewitching Tanya. But he continued to attend the weekly folk dances where he could see her, dance with her, talk with her, or, at the very least, listen to her as she talked with others.

Then, at a New Year's Eve party, he found himself alone with Tanya in an elevator. It was a festive occasion, with everyone in high spirits, and more than a little liquor had been consumed. Tanya was flushed with excitement and brimming with goodwill and friendliness. Impulsively, she reached out to Poddar and kissed him for the New Year. Poddar was stunned and awed. He had never had any physical contact with a woman other than mother, aunt, or grandmother, and now he had been kissed by Tanya. He was so overwhelmed that he almost immediately fled from her company to find Mistree and to tell him of this startling new development, this "wet kiss" that Tanya had bestowed upon him. He believed it was her definitive way of telling him that her true feelings were akin to his own.

In the months that followed, Poddar held on to the memory of that moment, for in it lay the revelation of what he believed to be the true state of affairs between him and Tanya. Tanya's behavior often confused him, for it was not always consistent with what he "knew" to be true: she cared for him. But she often broke dates without explanations or did not show up when expected; she talked in his presence of other men and her involvement with them; and she ignored him for entire evenings. And yet, she also allowed herself to display her "true feelings" toward him by dancing with him, calling him, and going to his room for long talks that were occasionally concluded with her kissing him good-bye.

The inconsistencies were something Poddar did not understand—Tanya was sending some message that he was not receiving. He installed microphones in his room so that he could record their conversations, both on the phone and when she came to see him. He then listened to their talks over and over again in order to clarify in his own mind the truth of her feelings. As he sat in his darkened room listening to her voice and her words, his doubts grew, but his need to quell those doubts grew faster and the reels of tape began to accumulate as he sought clearer evidence.

To listen to the tapes required time and Poddar began to skip his classes, then his work, then his meals. Finally, all his waking time was devoted to the study of the tape recordings of Tanya Tarasoff's conversations with him. The same single-minded diligence that had propelled him up the ladder of the Indian educational system was applied to the study of the nature of Tanya's feelings. But the study was inconclusive since there were clear inconsistencies. Mistree was consulted, asked to listen to portions of the tapes, and to give his opinion. Mistree, his friend and adviser who even in India had been called upon to teach Poddar the first of his social graces, listened and gave his advice. He counseled Poddar to meet with Tanya and, in a graceful way, tell her that he must not see her anymore, that she must not call him or try to see him, that his work must come before anything else. Mistree was perplexed by Poddar's obsession with Tanya and was certain that Tanya had only the most casual interest in his friend, but he could not persuade Poddar of that. He thought that Poddar would come to his senses only if he stopped seeing Tanya entirely. Poddar agreed reluctantly that such was the appropriate course. He met with Tanya, spoke as Mistree had advised, and returned to his room, his studies, his work. It was over.

A month passed and Poddar, relieved but regretful, went back to his work. He had been so concerned about Tanya and her feelings for him that he had been obliged to withdraw from all his winter quarter classes. When the spring quarter began in March, he once again settled down to his work. He avoided the weekend dances and other places where he might see Tanya. Then, one evening, she called. She told him she missed seeing him and talking with him, and asked if they couldn't be friends. He resisted, remembering his work. Mistree had advised him correctly, but perhaps they could simply be friends? He considered. He yielded. And Tanya reentered his life.

Another month passed and Poddar had returned to his darkened room, his tape recorder endlessly spinning out his moments with Tanya. He could not understand why she had called him back into her life if, when he responded, she had become as elusive as before. His obsession with discovering Tanya's true feelings about him expanded, taking up all his waking time. He saw that nothing else mattered and despaired of his state. Why was she doing this to him? Perhaps he had not made his feelings entirely clear to her. He must make one more effort. Meeting Tanya at a bus stop one rainy day in

March, he proposed marriage. To his consternation, Tanya did not accept his offer—nor did she refuse it. He had expected that she would at least say yes or no and his mind would be clear about his future. Poddar returned to his room, to his tapes, to an increasing sense of bitter rejection, and the dawning knowledge that soon everyone would know in what low regard he was held by Tanya Tarasoff.

Soon afterward he told Mistree of the ill-fated proposal, his bitter anger against Tanya, and the smirks and laughs that Tanya's friends were now directing toward him. Mistree was embarrassed by Poddar's remarks; he smiled awkwardly, trying to hide his uneasiness. But Poddar saw the smile and realized that even his oldest, most-trusted friend was not-so-secretly enjoying his disgrace. "Even you, Mistree," he said, "laugh at my state. But I am like an animal. I could do anything, I could kill her. If I killed her, what would you do?"

Mistree, stunned by these revelations, could only respond, "I would tell the truth."

"Then," replied Poddar, "I would have to kill you too." And he turned away, leaving Mistree alone in the hallway.

That evening, as Mistree was preparing for bed, there was a knock on his door. He answered and found Poddar, his eyes glazed as if he were not aware of what he was doing.

"Mistree, I have thought about it and you are my oldest friend. I could not kill you if I had to look in your eyes, see you dying. So I shall do it at night when I cannot see. Protect yourself, my friend; I am an animal."

Before Mistree could answer, Poddar disappeared down the hall, leaving Mistree confused and frightened at the blank look in his friend's eyes and at his words. He could not fathom the events of the day, but before he retired he pushed a heavy chair in front of the door.

Poddar stayed in his room for days. Sometimes there was a sign on the door saying "Do Not Disturb." At other times, the sign was down, and Mistree would go in and bring canned food to Poddar if he had not eaten, or would just stop to talk to him for a few minutes. Poddar did not mention murder again. Mistree believed that the constant listening to the tapes of Tanya's conversations was the continuing source of Poddar's problem. He tried to get Poddar to let him take the tapes but the attempt was unsuccessful. Eventually, Mistree did receive the tapes, and by that time, there was a ten-inch stack of reel-to-reel recordings, an estimated forty hours of conversation.

Finally, in the spring of 1969, Poddar returned to work, but when he was there, much of his time was spent sitting alone in a model of a ship's hull, one occasionally used for structural testing. He spoke on two occasions to fellow workers, telling them of his despair and of his bitterness. He also told them that he would like to blow up the house where Tanya lived with her parents and her brother Alex. Or perhaps he would blow up the whole block where she lived. His co-workers persuaded him that such actions were not possible, but they did not warn anyone or call the police. Poddar made no attempt to gather explosives after these conversations. He only sat in the darkened hull of the boat and thought about the ruin of his life.

Mistree spoke with him often in the evenings, trying to encourage him to attend to his studies and his work and talking of their life in India, hoping that by reminding him of a happier time Poddar would come to his senses. In June Tanya returned to Brazil for summer vacation; Mistree hoped that her absence would also help Poddar, as it had earlier when Poddar had broken off their meetings.

But there was little change. Hesitantly at first, Mistree suggested to Poddar that perhaps a doctor could help him with his troubled thoughts. In fact, he pointed out, there were doctors there at the campus for students to see. Reluctantly, Poddar was persuaded of the possibility, but he insisted that Mistree make the appointment and go with him to see this doctor.

Mistree promptly called the health services and spoke

with Dr. Stuart Gold. He told Gold of Poddar's troubles, of the death threats Poddar had made against Tanya and Mistree himself, and urged Dr. Gold to help his friend. An appointment was made and in early July, Mistree and Poddar arrived at Dr. Gold's office. As Poddar sat silently in a chair, Mistree began to explain Poddar's situation to the psychiatrist. Poddar neither assented to nor challenged Mistree's presentation, but merely sat as if his mind were elsewhere. After the basic facts had been presented, Dr. Gold suggested that perhaps Mistree would like to wait outside while he spoke with Poddar. Alone with the doctor and prodded by his questioning, Poddar became more responsive. Yes, it was all as Mistree had said. He could not eat, sleep, work, or do his studies. Yes, he had many tape recordings—of his conversations with a girl who had rejected him. He did not want to tell the doctor the girl's name. He hesitated to tell the doctor anything important for fear that others would find out about him. Dr. Gold told him his behavior was very disturbed, that in fact it was quite crazy, and gave him prescriptions for an antipsychotic drug and for a sleeping medication. He set up a series of weekly appointments and expected Poddar to return for them.

Dr. Gold was a psychiatrist on the in-patient service at the hospital. When the receptionists made appointments for new patients who called in, they usually made them with doctors in the out-patient department. Sometimes, if a caller sounded particularly disturbed and the receptionist thought the appointment might result in a hospital admission, one of the doctors from the in-patient service was scheduled to meet with the client. Mistree's call to the hospital had apparently triggered such a concern, but Dr. Gold, despite his telling Poddar that he thought his behavior was crazy, did not feel that Poddar needed to be kept in the hospital.

He did, however, feel that Poddar needed treatment for his serious problems. As Dr. Gold pointed out at the trial, he didn't usually prescribe antipsychotic drugs and tell patients they were crazy on their first visit. Dr. Gold arranged for

Poddar to see Dr. Lawrence Moore, a clinical psychologist from the outpatient department of the hospital. Weekly meetings were arranged.

Poddar kept the appointment with Dr. Moore and told him of his problems with Tanya, though he did not tell Dr. Moore her name. He did speak of his anger toward her and of his frequent desire to harm her, even to kill her. Poddar met weekly with Dr. Moore, but he distrusted him, believing that Dr. Moore might betray him. Poddar made another appointment with Dr. Gold and explained his distrust of Moore. Couldn't he see Dr. Gold? Or someone he could trust? Dr. Gold explained to Poddar that these feelings were not uncommon in therapy and that it was best if the doctor and the client work out the differences together. He sent Poddar back to Dr. Moore and Poddar reluctantly returned. Poddar saw Dr. Moore regularly for a total of eight sessions, but his distrust of the psychologist increased as Poddar became convinced that Moore would not protect him nor his secrets.

During these summer months, Poddar had struck up a close acquaintance with Alex Tarasoff, Tanya's younger brother. Both men were interested in electronics and, as Poddar struggled to regain his balance in life, Alex both helped him back to his studies and supplied a tenuous line to Tanya. They planned to find an apartment that they could share beginning in the fall. Poddar thought Tanya might move in with them. Alex often stayed in Poddar's room at the I-House during this period, and he seemed to replace Mistree as Poddar's closest friend. Mistree saw less and less of Poddar and, finally, by the first of September, when Poddar and Alex moved out, Mistree had lost almost all contact.

Visions of Tanya were also a part of Poddar's new life. He began to form a plan in which he would rescue Tanya from a terrible situation—one that he himself would arrange. (When Tanya recognized him as her savior—she would not know that she was also his victim—she would realize the strength of his devotion, the quality of his love, and the extent of her real need for him.) To achieve this plan, Podder would need a gun or two. He told Mistree of the planned gun purchase, though he did not explain to him its purpose. Mistree came to his own conclusions.

The news of Poddar's plan to purchase a gun certainly dimmed Mistree's hopes that therapy would restore Poddar's mind. Mistree's friendship with Poddar had become increasingly difficult to maintain. They had talked together about the therapy sessions with Dr. Moore. Poddar had insisted that Moore could not be trusted. He particularly feared that Moore would turn him in to the authorities. Finally, Poddar's fears of betrayal at the hands of Dr. Moore became so intense that he felt he had to break off the therapy. He told Mistree of this decision just as he had told him of the plan to buy a gun.

Mistree was deeply concerned that Poddar would fall into worse straits if he ceased meeting with the psychologist. Things did not seem to be going well, but they could be even worse. Mistree tried to persuade Poddar to continue with Dr. Moore, but his arguments did not seem to be very successful. Finally, Mistree called Dr. Moore and told him of Poddar's threats to stop the therapy sessions and of his plans to purchase a gun.

Moore found this news deeply disturbing. During the therapy sessions Poddar had made threats against Tanya. Although he was sometimes quite lucid, at other times he was very disturbed, and at these times he had made clear his desire to kill Tanya. Moore met with Poddar for what turned out to be the last time. The therapist conveyed the message to Poddar that he would have to take steps to restrain him if he continued to talk about killing Tanya. Poddar never returned for another appointment. His fears of betrayal seemed realized and he withdrew from the relationship. Shortly afterward, he moved from the I-House into an apartment with Alex Tarasoff. Neither Mistree nor Dr. Moore saw him again for many weeks.

Dr. Moore consulted with Dr. Gold about events in Poddar's treatment and it was decided that steps should be taken to confine him. Dr. Moore wrote a letter to the university police, which stated, in part,

> His mental status varies considerably. At times he appears to be quite rational, at other times he appears quite psychotic. It is my impression that currently the appropriate diagnosis for him is paranoid schizophrenic reaction, acute and severe. He is at this point a danger to the welfare of other people and himself. That is, he has been threatening to kill an unnamed girl who he feels has betrayed him and has violated his honor. He has told a friend of his (Farrokhg Mistree, also of International House) that he intends to go to San Francisco to buy a gun and that he plans to kill the girl. He has been somewhat more cryptic with me, but has alluded strongly to the compulsion to "get even with," and "hurt" the girl.
>
> I have discussed this matter with Dr. Gold and we concur in the opinion that Mr. Poddar should be committed for observation in a mental hospital. I request the assistance of your department in this matter.

In time the Berkeley campus police tracked down Poddar at his new apartment and, finding both young men at home, interviewed Poddar in Alex's presence. Poddar denied he had a weapon, and denied any specific threats, although he did acknowledge that there had been a troubled relationship between him and a young woman. The police warned him to stay away from her and left without taking any other action. Alex was present during this interview and knew that the supposed threats were against his sister Tanya. But he did not take them seriously and did not report them to his family.

In September Tanya returned from South America. Poddar again attended the Friday night folk dances where he could watch Tanya and occasionally speak with her. He kept his distance, carefully observing her manner, conversation, and style. One night he listened intently from a slight distance as she told a group of friends about her adventures in Brazil and her summer affair with a dashing Argentinian playboy-bootlegger. Poddar noted her pleasure in recounting the details of her amorous adventure and of the charms of her rich lover. Her voice resonated as if she were speaking into a microphone. Listening to her, Poddar felt as if Tanya was telling the story directly to him, to demonstrate once again her awful power over his feelings. Her cruelty to him was inexplicable.

He continued to see her and to speak with her. He began to follow her about on the college campus. He hung around her house. He became a spectral presence, always somewhere near, plaguing and frightening her. And he purchased a gun, perhaps to further his plan of rescuing her from a disastrous situation. He carried the gun with him sometimes, even though the plan was not yet ready.

He consulted with Alex about what would be the best way to approach his sister. Alex recommended that he stay away from her, that he not bother with her, that it was all over and best forgotten. But Poddar insisted that he must talk to Tanya, just to get things straight. Alex insisted that it was a bad idea. One day they began to argue about Poddar's insistence on seeing Tanya, and Alex shoved Poddar into the wall. Surprised that things had gotten so out of hand, they stopped the brawl and Alex relentingly gave one piece of advice to Poddar: Don't see Tanya at home if their father was around. Alex warned him that Mr. Tarasoff was hot-tempered, did not like guys fooling around with Tanya, and was likely to beat him up. All in all, Alex advised, it was a bad deal. Better to stay away from Tanya altogether.

Poddar was unable to sleep that night, and early the next morning, on October 27, he arose, dressed, and planned his trip to Tanya's home. Alex had already left the apartment. Poddar planned to arrive at Tanya's home after her father had left for work and before she left for school. This would be the last conversation he would have with her. He would find out why she behaved so unkindly to him and, understanding that, he would be free of her and her memory at last. As he began to get ready to leave, his ambivalence began to grow. His anger was so great that he was afraid he might harm her, but he felt he must see her in order to finish things between them. He decided he would go after all, but he took a gun and bullets with him, keeping them in his pockets.

As he walked up to Tanya's door, she saw him from her room where she was getting ready to leave for school. She asked her mother to answer the door and tell him she had already left. Her mother answered the door, talked to the sullen, insistent young man who never took his hands from his pockets, and assured him that Tanya had already left for school. Sensing some darkness in the situation, the mother found herself speaking angrily. She urged Poddar not to come back to their house again; better yet, he should go all the way back to India. He should not bother the Tarasoffs again.

Poddar returned to his apartment and to his bed. He began to brood about his miserable situation, and thought of reasons why he shouldn't kill Tanya. He also thought he heard Tanya talking to him. In midafternoon, he resolved to return to the house, hoping to speak to Tanya before anyone else came home. The thought of her wrathful father coming upon him was sobering, however, and he hesitated. Then the need to do what must be done came over him, and as he left his apartment, he slipped a kitchen knife as well as the gun into his pocket as protection against the avenging father.

He tried to call Alex before he left, but with no success. As he left their apartment, the manager saw him, said hello, and Poddar replied. When he arrived at Tanya's house, he looked about for signs of her father's car. Alex's description of the wrath of Mr. Tarasoff had had its effect upon him. But there was no sign of the terrifying father.

Poddar rang the bell. Tanya opened the door and asked what he wanted. She urged him to go away, told him that she didn't want to see him. In any case, she pointed out that her father would be home momentarily and would be very angry to see Poddar hanging about the house. Poddar tried to explain his need to talk to her, to find out why she had acted as she had toward him and why his affection had merited such cruelty. As he struggled with the words, he also struggled to reach out to her and force his way past the closing door. He gained entrance, but Tanya started to run away. He pursued her, still trying to explain what he needed from her. Just as he reached out to touch her, she screamed and her scream pushed him away. He had the gun in his hand and he fired at her scream. She ran again, now toward the front door, and the scream and the sound of the gun carried him with her toward the door. He took the knife from his pocket and as they plunged together through the door, he reached out again for her, touched her, held her. On the ground, at his feet, Poddar suddenly saw the knife. It was sticking in something. He staggered back as a whirlwind of impressions coursed through his mind. He thought the knife was sticking in Tanya. He dialed the phone number of the Berkeley city police. He thought he had killed someone.

Poddar was arraigned and charged with first-degree murder. The trial proceeded slowly. That he had stabbed Tanya Tarasoff to death was not disputed. He pled insanity and diminished capacity. The jury heard from Tanya's parents, Alex Tarasoff, Farrokhg Mistree, and Dr. Gold and Dr. Moore, as well as from others with less significant information. They heard from psychiatrists who interviewed Poddar after the killing. They considered the possibility of his being legally insane, but were not entirely persuaded of that likelihood. The psychiatric testimony was impressive to a degree: it stressed the diagnosis of paranoid schizophrenia. One psychiatrist had examined Poddar within twenty-four hours of the murder. He was a Berkeley police consultant and even he agreed that Poddar was a paranoid schizophrenic. But it was not enough. The jury found Poddar guilty of second-degree murder, that is, murder without premeditation. Poddar was sent to a California state prison and began to serve an indeterminate sentence that was likely to last about five years.

After Poddar's conviction, his case was appealed. He had a new lawyer, but one with no previous criminal experience because he had only recently been admitted to the bar. In preparing his brief for the appellate court, the lawyer noted many aspects of the trial that, in his opinion, merited a reversal of the verdict and a rehearing of the case. One of his last thoughts was that the judge had failed to give a particular and specific instruction to the jury about the meaning of diminished capacity. It was not particularly surprising that the instruction had not been given since neither attorney had ever requested it. But it became the principal objection to the trial process, buttressed by every conceivable additional point that might help obtain a reversal.

Five years after Poddar had begun serving his sentence in a California prison, the California Supreme Court issued its decision on Poddar's appeal. They overturned the jury verdict on the grounds that the trial judge had given inadequate instructions on diminished capacity to the jury. The obscure point had triumphed for some reason and a new trial was ordered.

The attorney who had represented the state before the Supreme Court was dismayed. He knew the difficulties of retrying a case, especially when so much time had passed since the crime. After six years, witnesses would be difficult to locate and, even if they were found, memories would be weak. Time often alters perceptions, and a victim that has been dead for six years would garner little sympathy. And yet, the case had to be retried. The task promised no pleasure, even if the state managed to convict Poddar again. It was hard enough to prove the state of a man's mind months after he had killed another person; years after, it might well prove impossible. Poddar might even get off entirely, by being found not guilty by reason of insanity. Despondently, the prosecutor began his preparations for a new trial.

Poddar's appellate attorney, the young man newly admitted to the bar, was as surprised as the prosecuting attorney was by his victory. But he was riding the crest and, having no more desire to retry a six-year-old case than the prosecution had, he decided to try for a further victory. He offered a compromise. Poddar had already served five years, he pointed out, and that was the average term that anyone served on a second-degree murder conviction. Even if the district attorney won the case on a retrial, Poddar was likely to be eligible for immediate parole on the basis of time already served. Why put everyone to the trouble of a new trial? If the state would agree to release Poddar from prison, the attorney would personally guarantee that Poddar would be on the next plane to India and would never return to the United States.

The attorney general's office of the state of California considered the offer. It had substantial merit, and it was true that Poddar had been a model prisoner. He probably would be released immediately, even if convicted in a second trial. Enough was enough. The deal was struck.

Poddar was released, and his attorney escorted him to the San Francisco airport where he boarded a plane to Calcutta. He returned to India, resumed his life, and married a lawyer. No more is known, for he refuses all attempts at communication from Americans.

Thus Poddar was never found guilty of the murder of Tanya Tarasoff, nor was he declared insane. Although he did serve some prison time, he was not deported at his release. He was sent home, like a bad boy. But his record is, in a legal sense, clean.

The companion case, *Tarasoff* v. *Regents of the University of California*, ended with the same kind of inconclusiveness. Tanya's parents sued the University of California for the psychiatrist's failure to warn them or Tanya of the danger that Poddar posed to the family. But before this case reached the trial stage, it was appealed to the California Supreme Court on a technical question. After the first decision was rendered by the supreme court, a rehearing was requested.

Such a request is almost never granted, but it was in this case, and a second and different decision was issued on the question of whether a therapist had any responsibility to warn others when a patient seemed dangerous.

The first decision said that both the police and the therapist were legally responsible for protecting threatened third parties, but the second decision declared that while the police did not have such a duty, the psychotherapist does have a legal responsibility to take appropriate action when he believes his patient may be dangerous to others. They indicated that such an action may include informing those whom the therapist believes may best avert the intended harm (such as the threatened victim, the police, or others). Seven years after Tanya's death the *Tarasoff* case was now ready to be brought to trial. Poddar, by this time, had been released from prison. Since Poddar had not finally been held legally responsible, were the therapists, Dr. Gold and Dr. Moore, going to be held responsible for Tanya's death?

As with the ordered retrial of Poddar, the trial in the *Tarasoff* litigation never took place. The Tarasoffs and the regents of the university concluded an out-of-court settlement whose terms were never officially disclosed. It is rumored that the money involved was minimal.

Thus, after years of litigation and the expenditure of thousands of dollars and thousands of hours, the quest for legal responsibility in the murder of Tanya Tarasoff was concluded. No one was found guilty, no one was found responsible, and no one was found to have failed in any duty they might have had to prevent Tanya's sad death.

Such a result seems remarkable in the light of events. This was a murder that might have been prevented at a dozen points, but it ends by being a death with no reason and no responsibility. The results of the legal process may be attributed to the criminal law system's great difficulty in handling the question of individual responsibility when behavior strays from cultural and psychological norms.

The actions of the California Supreme Court in these

two cases are puzzling. Usually in a case where guilt is so clear—that is, commission of the criminal action itself is unquestioned—technical objections are unlikely to win reversals unless the technical issue is one particularly embroiled in civil rights questions or is a particularly egregious procedural error. In both cases, the expectation is that the accused will probably be found guilty again, but that the police and the judicial system will in the future be more careful about their handling of such cases. The surprising reversal of Poddar's criminal conviction on such an unlikely technical issue suggests that the court was unhappy with the verdict itself and had only this technical ground to force another hearing of the case.

It is not unlikely that when the supreme court received the brief appealing Poddar's conviction and read the transcript of the trial, they believed that Poddar was mentally disturbed and that either an insanity acquittal or a diminished capacity finding (reducing the charge to voluntary manslaughter) was an appropriate result. If so, a reversal focusing on the diminished capacity instructions to the jury would make either verdict more obtainable.

Certainly it is not only jurors who are hard pressed to deal reasonably with these difficult questions pertaining to a defendant's state of mind. The justices are also capable of being humanly touched by the anguish and confusion of people's lives. Their sympathy and empathy for Poddar may well have led them to make this unlikely reversal.

The attorney general's decision to release Poddar and to avoid a further trial was no doubt affected by his realization that the diminished capacity plea might find favor with a new jury and that Poddar would be unlikely to be imprisoned any longer regardless of a jury verdict. His decision was one of practicality and efficiency. Why expend time and money if the only possible positive outcome would be a symbolic one? Although such a decision is understandable, the power of symbols should never be underestimated.

One important question in this part of the *Poddar-Tarasoff* case is whether the supreme court's decision to reverse the criminal verdict against Poddar affected their attitudes when they came to decide upon the Tarasoffs' suit against the University of California. If, after reading the Poddar transcript, they felt Poddar was seriously mentally disturbed —and such a conclusion would be an easy one to arrive at—they might have been inclined to shift the moral responsibility for the murder, along with some sense of legal responsibility, to the therapists and to the police. If we see the murder of Tanya Tarasoff as a preventable crime, then the next question to ask is: Who should have prevented it?

The decisions in the *Tarasoff* case suggest that the supreme court justices thought *someone* was responsible. It was not Poddar, for they had already reversed his conviction. In the first *Tarasoff* decision they suggested that the therapists and the police were the guilty parties. By the time of the second decision, they had settled on the therapists only as the prime candidates for responsibility in the death of Tanya Tarasoff.

But even then, pronouncement of guilt and apportionment of responsibility was never made, for by making an out-of-court settlement, the university and the therapists avoided the risk of being found liable (although, as one justice commented, the therapists might in fact have done as much as could be legally required of them, so a "not guilty" verdict could have resulted from a trial).

That Poddar exhibited very strange behavior is not questioned by anyone involved in this case. But even so, why should he bear no legal guilt? If he had been found guilty but with a diminished capacity finding, he would probably have served far less time than the five years he did spend in prison. The Supreme Court reversal suggests that that would have been fairer. But would it have been?

Is the question of Poddar's state of mind really relevant to his guilt? Or is it more relevant to what should be done with him by way of treatment or prison rehabilitation? Like the other defendants in this book, Poddar was under great emotional stress. In addition, he had to contend with the problem of cultural alienation and adaptation. It was an extremely difficult time for him but he functioned well enough. He was sufficiently competent to procure guns and ammunition, to conceive plots and make plans, to rent apartments and deal with a roommate.

Poddar's story is filled with pathos; it is a story dominated as well by a feeling that "none of this was necessary"—not his despair, not Tanya's death. It was all a misunderstanding. These were ordinary people in situations where the emotional pitch was too high for them. By the time of the appeal, Poddar must have appeared like a high-wire trapeze artist working without a net. When he fell, sympathy flowed out toward him. The audience didn't remember that he had chosen to take those risks.

The judicial system intervened in this case to try to improve upon the trial court's allocation of guilt and responsibility. Their efforts were rough and, in the long run, counterproductive, because no one was found guilty and no one was held responsible. The psychiatric testimony doubtless influenced the jury, resulting in a verdict of second- rather than first-degree murder. It doubtless influenced the supreme court justices, resulting in a reversal on technical grounds. It doubtless influenced the attorney who decided to release Poddar to India. But even if the psychiatrists had not testified at the trial, the impact of Poddar's mental state would have been felt. Mistree's observations were powerful statements about Poddar's irrationality. There was ample evidence of Poddar's disturbed perception of events. It would probably have made little difference if there had been no psychiatric testimony about capacity to form intent, for Poddar's disturbed state was readily apparent to all.

What would have made a difference in this case would have been a way for the jury and the court to separate the question of Poddar's guilt and the question of what should become of him. It would have helped if they had not been required to decide whether he was sane or insane. He was both. As Dr. Moore pointed out, sometimes he was quite lucid and sometimes he was quite disturbed. The lucidity and the disturbance of his thoughts came together and led to the murder of Tanya Tarasoff. The jury found him sane; the Supreme Court seemed to think him insane. Poddar went home with an unexpected exoneration supplied by the machinations of the judiciary.

The practical results of *Poddar* and *Tarasoff* seem to represent the legal system's awkward attempts to balance claims and to assign responsibility when it is unhappy with the judgment of the jury. It has a quality of rough justice although it is not perhaps the best conclusion or the just ending we would prefer. But it is far more defensible than the conclusions reached in many other cases where neither moral nor practical responsibility is achieved. In the murder of Tanya Tarasoff, punishment was achieved outside the legal rulings, but a legal system that must circumvent itself to find justice is a system in severe need of reform.

LEONARD SMITH

Indiana Death Trip

In the summer of 1978 Lyman Bostock really seemed to have it made. He was one of the two or three highest paid players ever in American League baseball. He was highly regarded by the sportswriters and by the baseball fans. It didn't help. He was a golden boy, but he was murdered with a twelve-gauge shotgun at 10:30 P.M. at Fifth and Jackson in downtown Gary, Indiana, while he was riding in the back seat of his uncle's Buick. The man who shot him was Leonard Smith, a thirty-three-year-old unemployed truck driver. Leonard Smith had never seen Lyman Bostock before that night—he may not really have seen him even when he shot him, and it is sure he never knew it was *the* Lyman Bostock. But maybe that didn't matter. If Leonard Smith had sat down and coolly and deliberately selected someone to shoot in order to even the score for his miserable life, he could scarcely have picked a more appropriate victim. Leonard Smith had dreamed of going as far up as Lyman Bostock had gone. Lyman went right up every step that Leonard Smith ever tried—but somehow, for Leonard, with every attempt he ended up two steps back. Bostock was a winner, Smith was a loser. As a loser, Leonard Smith was in severe anguish. His lawyer was amazed at the frustration that the man had endured and surely, he said, here was a man at the end of his rope. We can understand, the attorney counseled the jury, how he came to kill Lyman Bostock and we can understand why he was not responsible.

To the psychiatrist who examined him, Leonard Smith was an absolutely tragic figure: a man who tried and tried at a dream of a better life, with a wife, children, a house with a yard and fence, a good job—to be safe and secure, warm and loving, forever and ever. But for Leonard, the dream was always thwarted: by his wife, by his employers, by racial prejudice, and by life itself.

But, with the strange twists that life, the criminal justice system, and psychiatric expert witnesses provide, when Lyman Bostock ran out of luck, Leonard Smith ran into it. Bostock's hot success turned cold that night as he drove down Fifth Avenue and got a shotgun blast in the head. Leonard Smith's bleak past picked up, if only briefly, because twenty-one months after the shooting he walked out of jail after receiving four months of psychiatric treatment and three months of evaluation. He had a not guilty by reason of insanity verdict in his pocket.

To get that verdict, Smith had to go through two trials. In the first, a three-day trial, the jury members were irresolvably divided about his guilt, and a new trial had to be started. Two psychiatrists, Dr. Frank Hogle and Dr. Lee Michael Periolat, testified at the first trial. Dr. Hogle had seen Leonard off and on for about three months; Dr. Periolat had seen him twice and only briefly each time. Both testified that he was, in their opinion, legally sane. In Indiana, the standard for absence of criminal responsibility was that the accused, at the time of the crime and as a result of a mental disease or defect, must lack substantial capacity either to appreciate the wrongfulness of his conduct or to conform his conduct to the requirements of the law. Dr. Hogle had doubts about his judgment that Smith was legally sane; Dr. Periolat was more certain that Leonard was sane. During the second trial, Dr. Frank Brogno, a psychologist, was brought in, and he thought Leonard was insane, incapable of resisting the urge to kill, and had machine-scored tests to back him up. The jury succumbed to his blandishments, his tests, and his opinion. They were able to see Leonard as Dr. Hogle saw him, as a man with "gradually increasing neurotic difficulties" or, as Smith's attorney phrased it, a man whose "repeated failures . . . slowly eroded his functions." With his mental functions gone and his *control* of his functions gone, "he would not be able to conform his conduct to the requirements of the law. Isn't that true?" asked the attorney. "That's possible," replied Dr. Hogle. Of course. *Anything* is possible. The Chicago Cubs winning the pennant is possible. But the second jury in *People* v. *Smith* found Leonard Smith's insanity, his lack of criminal responsibility for Lyman Bostock's death more than possible; they thought it was true, though they never heard a word from Leonard about it.

That Leonard Smith had a troubled life cannot be doubted. But there is no principle of criminal law or of American jurisprudence that suggests that culpability for crimes is to be measured by the hardness of the violator's life. Such a view would inevitably contain its opposite: Lyman Bostock's murder would be acceptable because Lyman had had too good a life. Together, Bostock and Smith would balance each other out.

Such a view is clearly offensive, but it is equally clear that the jury and the psychiatrists were significantly touched in some way by Leonard Smith and his hard luck story. Perhaps, for that jury, Bostock was too golden—a celebrity, a success, a man with a big contract and a big future. And then, he wasn't at the trial. He was long buried, beyond help or sympathy. The jury could not very well identify with Bostock, but they could with Leonard Smith. They could understand the struggles he had been through, the losses he had survived. Dr. Hogle, privy to Leonard's confidence during the many sessions they had in the winter of 1978 and spring of 1979, told them of Leonard's desperate attempts through the years to keep on believing that this was a fair world, one in which he could make it if he would try hard and keep on trying. How could the jurors strike down a man so sincere and so dedicated to trying? When the psychiatrists told the jury that he was legally sane, they could not find him guilty. But when a new, expert opinion was delivered during the second trial, the jurors were free to vote their feelings and thereby sanction Leonard Smith's struggles.

His struggles began early on. As he himself described it during the first trial, he was puzzled and uneasy when, as a child, he realized that he and his five brothers and sisters had among them four last names. He "didn't like it and didn't understand it," all this divorcing and separating. His own father had left when he was but three years old, too young even to remember his being there; two of the other fathers seem never even to have moved in. True, the fourth one was there, but what was he to make of all these disappearing fathers? How could they be a family if the fathers kept wandering off?

As a teenager, Leonard sought out his own natural father and went to live with him, but that didn't work out at all. His father had a new wife and family. The new family had no place for Leonard, and the new wife had no yearning for a grownup son from the past. Leonard felt he had a special kind of relationship with his father, but the new wife resented it. Leonard left and moved back with his mother, deeply saddened at his inability to make a lasting bond with his dad. He later returned to his father's home again, to try one more time to make it work, but again, according to Leonard, he was shut out by the new family and the new wife, and he returned to his mother's home a final time to contemplate the inability of fathers to stay with their children—and perhaps to brood upon how women made it impossible for fathers to stay with their children.

As he grew older, he continued to see the disarray of broken families around him and the damage that these separations brought. It was as if, in Leonard's imagination, the family partings were not simply the comings and goings of people. Instead, they were the tearing apart of a single unit. Thus, the departure of his father had been achieved only by ripping him out of the family group, and all those in the family who had been near him were left torn and bleeding by this act. Leonard, according to the psychiatric version, bled throughout his life.

Two of Leonard's sisters, according to Leonard's own version of his life, also suffered grievously from this destruction of the family unit. Leonard had been the youngest of three children in his mother's marriage to Leonard's father. The two older children were daughters, Andrea and Joyce. Leonard's intense feelings about family doubtless gave him a greater feeling of belonging with these two sisters than he experienced with his two half-brothers or with his half-sister. As a result, Andrea and Joyce's fate seemed to him inextricably bound up with his own, their choices a proof of his own version of reality.

By the time Leonard was a teenager, both Andrea and Joyce had married and were off with their own families. Andrea had two children, while Joyce had five. But marriage didn't work for them either and the fathers went away, leaving the wives and the children alone. Just after Leonard graduated from high school, he moved in with his sister Andrea and her two sons, at his mother's request. Andrea was having trouble; Leonard would take care of her. It was, perhaps, Leonard's first attempt to take on the care of another person entirely, and to fulfill his fantasies about men and fathers and what they could do to make everyone's life better. Leonard got a job; Andrea took care of the kids and the house. As

Leonard testified, "we split the responsibilities down the middle." But one day when Leonard came home from his job, he found that Andrea had laid down her half of the responsibilities. She was babbling incoherently. Leonard tried to understand what was happening, but Andrea only became louder, more incoherent, more excited. He fled to his mother's house for help.

Andrea was taken to an emergency hospital, but while there, she tried to jump out a window in an attempt to kill herself. They stopped her and treated her, but her condition became worse. The hospital was unable to help her and she was eventually committed to the Westville Psychiatric Hospital in Indiana.

Leonard's other sister, Joyce, had married and given birth to five children, but her marriage didn't work out either. Her husband—the father of five children—departed, leaving Joyce to take care of the children and the home. Joyce was under psychiatric care and on some kind of medication. Leonard never knew exactly what medicine it was that she took, but he knew his mother was always reminding her to keep taking the medicine. Joyce hadn't wanted to always be taking medicine. She wanted to have some fun, because she was lonely and young and didn't always want the responsibility for all those children.

Leonard would often come by Joyce's house during this time to help her out, trying to show her what she needed to do, how she could better take responsibility for her children, and how she could be a good mother for this family. But it didn't work. Joyce was always thinking she needed a husband. For about four years, Joyce struggled with her home, her children, her medication, her very life; and Leonard struggled with her. Finally, one day, she walked in front of a train, and all her struggles were over.

Leonard's sisters had both stopped trying. He could see that. Their fate was perhaps another message to him about what it took in this world to make it; how hard you had to try and how you had to keep on trying. But their fate was also a fearful prognostication to him about his own destiny and the possibility of his going crazy.

Leonard intended for his life to be a success. There was evidence all around him of how hard a job that would be. Success doesn't come easily to a man whose childhood home has been shattered; it doesn't come easily to a black man in Gary, Indiana, with only a high school education; it doesn't come easily to a man whose two full sisters had gone crazy. But he intended to *try* both with his work and with a family.

Soon after he graduated from high school he got a job as a member of a track gang with a local railroad company. He worked hard and was moved into a fireman's position, which was a good level of advancement for a young man. But Leonard had his eye on the driver's wheel, and he began to think about becoming a train engineer. That was a good job for a successful man to have; it would show that he was responsible, a real man.

About the same time as he was thinking about trying for an engineer's job, he met Barbara Smith. He was twenty-three when he first met her in 1968. Barbara said she was eighteen, but Leonard later learned that she was only seventeen. Lord knows why she'd lied about just that one year. She'd been living with an aunt, and Leonard had come by to visit a friend of his who was married to the aunt.

Leonard and Barbara hit it off right away and they started dating. He learned that Barbara was living with her aunt because her mother had put her out of the house when Barbara had given birth to a baby the previous year. Her mother, said Barbara, couldn't stand the shame and suggested that Barbara and the baby, Nicole, be on their way. Leonard liked Barbara and the baby, and thought that maybe he ought to be taking care of them. He asked to meet Barbara's father and mother, who were divorced, and Barbara introduced Leonard to them separately. About three months after they met, Leonard suggested that she and Nicole come live with him, and Barbara agreed.

Leonard went to work at the railroad each day and Barbara stayed home and took care of Nicole. Things seemed to be going pretty good for Leonard Smith. He had a good job, a pretty live-in girl friend, and a baby who, if she was not naturally his own daughter, would surely grow up thinking of him as her daddy.

Barbara had dropped out of school during her pregnancy and Leonard encouraged her to go back and finish high school. If she went to night school, he promised he would babysit. Leonard believed in getting a good education, and he was proud when Barbara went back to night school, then day school, and finally graduated. He went to her graduation and thought it a shame that no member of Barbara's family showed up. Unlike Leonard, Barbara's family didn't seem to place the same premium on bettering oneself. But Barbara would try, under Leonard's urging. She even tried college though it didn't work out. When Leonard recollected Barbara's attempts at college, he concluded with his persistent optimism, "She would never complete it, but she tried."

After high school, Barbara went to work in a nursing home, but she didn't like cleaning up after people, and the patients were too heavy for her to lift. All in all, it seemed an unpromising line of work and Leonard counseled her to stay at home if that's what she would like to do. He had a good job and was making good money, so there wasn't any reason why she should be doing work she didn't like. Barbara quit her job and Leonard took care of her and Nicole.

But life was seldom easy between them. Leonard wanted a perfect life with the father/husband in control and in command. He had an idea of how a "good" family operated, how children were to be raised, and how husbands and wives were to behave. If Barbara had any such conscious ideas, they were at least not the same as those of Leonard. To Barbara, he was just too heavy-handed in every way. When he didn't like how she acted, he came after her about it and frequently it ended in blows, she perhaps as much a participant in the violence as he, but at a decided disadvantage since she weighed about 100 to 110 pounds and Leonard was about 170 pounds.

Leonard had fractured her jaw once, and she had also suffered a concussion, plus the regular cuts, bruises, and swellings that result from violent arguments. Often she'd report him to the police, but usually nothing came of that. Sometimes Barbara would disappear for a few days, weeks, or even months after these arguments, but then they would talk, start dating again, and then she and Nicole would move back in with him. The family would be back together again with Leonard at the head of it.

Leonard's dream of becoming a railroad engineer had finally been realized during these years. It had not been easy or likely. Even in a city like Gary, where the large black population was sensing its political power, the really good jobs were usually kept for the whites. But Leonard persevered and eventually, after four years as a train fireman, he became a locomotive engineer. The catch—that his train ran out of Joliet, Illinois, a considerable distance from his home in Gary. But he took on the distance. The hardship spurred his ambition to overcome the obstacles that lay before him. One day, driving to work in a heavy winter storm, he did not make it to the yard on time. His train went out twenty minutes late. And Leonard Smith's brief locomotive engineer career was over.

In 1972 Leonard was still with the railroad but not with Barbara. As a result of one of their frequent disagreements they had separated, but this time, instead of trying to coax Barbara to come back, Leonard took up with somebody else, trying to get his life together without Barbara. The affair didn't work out, didn't even last long, but the young woman became pregnant. However, she didn't want anything to do with Leonard or for him to have anything to do with his child when it was born. She wouldn't even accept money, according to Leonard. He felt bad about this child of his who would come into the world without a father. On the other hand, Barbara wanted to come back and maybe she was ready to finally settle down.

Barbara returned and shortly afterward became pregnant. Then, in March 1973, about five years after they had first met, after countless separations and reconciliations, just after the birth of Leonard's first daughter by the departed girl friend, and just two months prior to the birth of his second daughter, Ebony, Leonard and Barbara were married.

By now, 1973, Leonard's railroad career was over and he had been obliged to reimagine his future. He saw carpentry as a good, honest line of work, but the fact that the carpenter's union had an unofficial rule that no blacks were to be admitted to the guild made it difficult to attain his goal. Leonard Smith had already overcome that issue when he became an engineer. He simply kept at it and was finally accepted into an apprentice program. Unfortunately the program was north of Chicago and the traveling from Gary became too much. It was just too far and no apprentice programs closer to home were available. The carpentry dream was over, too. Then he tried to enlist in the army. Twice he went down and twice he was rejected, but he never knew why. Whoever it was Uncle Sam wanted, it wasn't Leonard Smith.

The first five years of Barbara and Leonard's married life moved at a roller-coaster pace from 1973 to 1978. There continued to be problems with Leonard's work, but in addition to that, their family difficulties continued. They just couldn't seem to keep on an even keel and there were at least fifteen more separations. The birth of their second daughter, Nefertira, in 1975, didn't stabilize the family at all.

Barbara once took off for Florida to start a new life with her daughters, but that didn't work out. She then went to South Carolina where she had family, and although her relatives were willing to let her stay with them until she got on her feet, Barbara lost her zeal. She called Leonard and asked him for enough money so that she and the kids could fly back to Gary. Leonard was happy to hear she was coming back but sent her only enough for bus fare. Barbara returned, but she was in Gary for a week before she got around to moving back with Leonard.

Another time, Barbara moved out and filed charges with the police against Leonard after he had knocked her around a little too much. The police, as usual, hadn't taken much notice of the complaint and in time Barbara moved back in again. Some time later, Leonard was stopped for a moving traffic violation, and when the police checked him out, they found there was an arrest warrant out on him because of Barbara's complaint. They took him in, checked with Barbara to see if she still wanted to press charges, and, to everyone's surprise, she did.

Leonard ended up with a year's probation, and his first probation officer would sometimes see both Leonard and Barbara in an attempt to help them handle their problems. But their problems were formidable and somehow the probation officer started seeing Barbara on his off-duty time. Leonard couldn't imagine how such a thing could happen. The guy who was supposed to help him straighten up was chasing after his woman. Barbara left again and a new person became Leonard's probation officer.

During Leonard's trial, Barbara admitted to knowing his first probation officer, even spending some time with him. Yes, he had even bought some beds for her and the girls when they were burned out of an apartment they were staying in. But, said Barbara, none of that meant the probation officer was her boyfriend. Leonard knew better. Probation officers don't find apartments and buy furniture for ladies just because they're nice guys.

One day Barbara called Leonard to ask him to take care of the three little girls. Leonard was always happy to have the kids with him during Barbara's frequent departures. But the next day she called to say that she was off to California for a little vacation. There was no way Leonard would stand for that. She could live with him or let *him* keep the kids if she was leaving, but he sure wasn't going to babysit for her while she took off for Los Angeles with some other dude. He trotted the kids right back to the relatives that Barbara was staying with and left them on the doorstep. Barbara was on the phone soon enough, complaining about "How could he do that to her?" But Leonard knew he had to stand up for something. Eventually she came back to him again.

By now Leonard had settled on becoming a truck driver, and he had entered a federal job-training program. He completed the program successfully and went to work as a long-haul truck driver. He'd made it again. He had a good job and was making good money, but he was never home. Leonard wondered how he could be a good family man if he was never home. A father had to be with his children, not with his truck, when evening came. He quit the long-haul business and settled for driving a truck locally for a steel company.

Barbara was home, the children were there, and life settled down for a little while. In 1977, with Leonard still at his trucking job and the children getting a little older and less dependent, Barbara thought she might like to go back to school in order to get a good job. She started attending court reporter's school and she was doing all right. Leonard was proud of her. The girls were in school during the day and so was she.

In 1978, though, the steel company trucking job went sour. Leonard was fired from Inland Steel for making an illegal turn with a truck. He filed a union grievance against the company, denying the company's charges, but that would take time to hear.

In the meantime, he was just another black man in his mid-thirties, out of work and out of luck, with a string of jobs behind him that hadn't worked out. Leonard was still thinking things could come together. He could apply for a job as a city fireman in Gary. He and Barbara and the three children were going to be happy, a real family.

In the summer of 1978, when court reporter school let out, Barbara got a job at the nearby J. C. Penney. It would be just for the summer, but she could use the money and, since she had gone back to school, she was used to being out of the house and doing something. Sometimes she had to work nights and Leonard was never too partial to that. Since he had lost his job at Inland Steel and was around the house to take care of the kids, Barbara couldn't understand his feelings. But Leonard got tired of being alone, not knowing when Barbara would turn up, when she would finally get around to coming home after work.

One night, toward the end of the summer, Barbara was working until nine in the evening, and she told Leonard she planned to get a ride home with one of her uncles. Leonard began looking for her around nine-thirty, but Barbara didn't show. He waited. He fumed. And time passed. Leonard was getting awfully tired of Barbara's not even letting him know where she was.

At 2:00 A.M. (or at 11 P.M.—their respective stories differed at the trial), Barbara came home. Leonard was in a rage. Barbara couldn't see what the big deal was since she'd spent plenty of nights at home alone. Anyway, she had just stopped off with her uncle to have a drink (or several, plus a little dope, was Leonard's version). They argued. They fought. Barbara again made a plan to leave. This time, it would be the last.

In the morning Leonard's mother, who lived in the apartment on the floor below them, took the little girls off to a church social. Barbara left a message for her: would she please drop off the three girls at Barbara's mother's house after church? She did, and Barbara and the children were off again.

Leonard was depressed. He became more withdrawn. When Barbara and the kids were gone, he would stay alone in his room and brood about his life and family. His best friend noticed the change in him and tried to talk to him about it, but he finally just stopped coming around. Leonard didn't seem to want friends. He was obsessed with getting Barbara and the kids to return and with their being a family again.

On September 19, 1978, Barbara filed for a divorce. She had filed for divorce before, but this time it was going to be final. She didn't tell Leonard. She and the girls were staying with her sister Janice, and it was crowded. The girls were sleeping on the floor, but Barbara was used to these makeshift accommodations, and so were the girls.

Four days later—on September 23—Leonard called Barbara, hoping they could make some headway on getting back together. They talked for a couple of hours on the phone. There was no mention of divorce. Barbara wanted some sewing things she'd left in their apartment, and Leonard wanted a pair of his trousers that Barbara had. They decided to meet later in the day, to talk more and to exchange their belongings.

When Leonard arrived at Janice's place at around five or six o'clock, he was hoping to see not only Barbara but the kids as well. The trouble with Barbara's leaving—well, one trouble out of many—was that he never got to see the kids unless she decided it was okay. So he knew that even though he was there and the kids were there, she might not let him see them, let alone talk to them.

Barbara came to the door when he arrived, but she didn't ask him in. It didn't look good for seeing the kids. Leonard sat out on the steps while Barbara stood in the doorway. They talked for an hour, maybe two hours. They went over it all again, the whole ten years. He reminded her of the kids and that they needed to grow up right. He told her that he'd enrolled Ebony, now five, in a Catholic school. He wanted his little girl to go to a good school where she could learn the right things and how to make something of herself in life. But, he asked Barbara, how could Ebony grow up right, even if she went to a fine school, if she had no family, no daddy at home? Leonard pointed out several times to Barbara that he had actually enrolled Ebony in a private school, but the good life for Ebony couldn't happen if Barbara didn't come back to him.

Once during this long conversation Ebony came to the door. Leonard talked to her, hugged her, and told her not to worry, that everything was going to be all right, that they were all going to be back together very soon. Barbara again did not mention the divorce suit she had filed four days earlier, although she had ample opportunity during her two talks with Leonard that day. She never explained why. Maybe she was afraid. Maybe she was tired of the crowded conditions at Janice's house and was thinking of coming back.

Leonard finally left, feeling there was hope for them. As he later testified in court, with respect to his remarks to Ebony, he just felt things had to get better. He felt such sorrow for his little girl who couldn't possibly understand why all this was happening. Leonard just couldn't believe Barbara would tear them all apart. And maybe Barbara didn't believe it either and that's why she didn't tell him about the divorce.

And that was the state of Leonard Smith's life on September 23, 1978, the day that Lyman Bostock came to Chicago with the Angels to play baseball with the White Sox; the day that Lyman Bostock came to Gary, Indiana, to see some old friends and relatives.

In 1978 Bostock was really on a roll. That season he was playing the first year of a five-year contract with Gene Autry's California Angels, a contract that would net him at least $2.25 million over its term. He was collecting $450,000 a year, or almost $3,000 every time he stepped out onto the field to play a game.

But it wasn't just the money. Lyman was, as the baseball writers would say it, *some* kind of ballplayer, *some* kind of guy. He was steady, always in there hustling and playing with the team. He was also a public-spirited citizen, working off-season with ghetto kids in Los Angeles, hoping to help them find a better life.

He came by his talent naturally, his father having been a

famous ballplayer in the Negro American League. Lyman, a child of a different time, had been able to make it to *the* American League, and it had been a straight-line trip: high school, college, minor leagues, then up to the majors and the Minnesota Twins in 1975. Before moving to the Angels, Lyman played three seasons with the Twins and, in 1977, his last year there, hit .377, the second highest batting average in the American League that year. Four years in the majors, and he was at the top.

When he moved to the Angels the team had great hopes for him, but Lyman fell immediately into an unexplained slump. By mid-April of the 1978 season he was batting only 2 for 39. He was doing okay out in right field, but baseball teams don't pay over $2 million for an okay right fielder. Bostock was the subject of a *Chicago Tribune* editorial when he announced his decision not to accept his April paycheck if he didn't come out of his slump by the end of the month. The *Trib* thought it a pretty impressive stand and opined that Bostock was showing everyone what *real* accountability looked like.

Lyman did come out of his batting slump, and by mid-September was batting .294. He commented to a fellow player, "I got my life straightened out off the field and that turned it around for me on the field." He was right. Lyman Bostock's life was all together.

Lyman enjoyed it when the California Angels played the White Sox in Chicago because he could look forward to a big crowd of family supporters driving in the short distance from Gary, Indiana, to watch him play, cheer him on, and see how big he really had made it. Playing in California was good, where you were a hustling, happening member of a team whose fans really cared, but in Chicago it was different because the fans there included family—five uncles, three aunts, and an array of cousins and good friends.

In Chicago, Lyman would usually take as much time as he could to go down to Gary, to hang out with his relatives and friends. He'd get some good food, jazz around with the guys, cruise the streets a little, and visit around. He'd come home to Gary as the local boy who made good, and everybody was always glad to see him.

On September 23 about twenty-five of his relatives had been up to see him play—a real turnout. The Angels lost, but it was close, 5 to 4, and Lyman looked good at bat, hitting a solid two for four. After the game, he went to Gary with the family. He and his uncle, Tom Turner, drove around in Tom's 1976 Buick Limited, saw some folks, ate dinner, and drove around some more. It seemed like always, like a lot of good visits in Gary. But this time, this trip to Gary was to be different—it was a death trip for "Bones" Bostock. He was the wrong man, in the wrong place, at the wrong time. The roll he was riding came up snake eyes.

After the game, Lyman went down to Gary. He was driving around town with his uncle Tom Turner and they were reminiscing about how Lyman used to visit Gary when he was a teenager in high school. Tom had been going with a woman then who had several daughters. Lyman remembered one of those daughters fondly—Joan Hawkins. He remembered her as a little kid, eight or nine years old. He remembered joking with her and reading her some stories. She had been a great kid, but he wondered what she was like now. Tom hadn't seen Joan for a long time himself, so they decided to see if they could find her. They drove over to the place where her mother used to live. To Tom's surprise, Barbara Smith, Joan Hawkins's sister, answered the door. Tom had known all the daughters, Joan, Barbara, Carla, and Janice—when he'd been spending time with their mother. They used to call him their godfather.

Tom was glad to see Barbara and he introduced her to Lyman. Barbara gave them Joan's phone number and asked Tom for his so that, if she heard from Joan, she could have her get in touch with Tom and Lyman.

A flurry of phone calls followed Tom and Lyman's visit to the house. Barbara called around trying to get hold of

Joan, and when she did, Joan called Tom. Tom and Lyman met Joan, and they talked about old times, about how Joan didn't even remember Lyman from those days when he had come summer visiting and played with her. There wasn't all that much to talk about, but it was a friendly, hometown feeling. Joan had no car and needed a ride to Barbara's, as she, Barbara, and a cousin were going to a party that night and some of the clothes she needed were at Barbara's house. Lyman and Tom gave her a ride over and she suggested that they come in for a while. Afterward, they could give both Barbara and Joan a ride over to their cousin Betty's house.

Tom was amenable, but the fact was, his sister-in-law was right then fixing dinner for Lyman, and Tom wanted "Bones" to sit down to it while it was still hot. He suggested an alternative. Joan should take his sister-in-law's phone number and when she was ready to go to give him a call. They would come back and give her and Barbara a ride. Joan agreed and Tom and Lyman went off for a family dinner.

Barbara had been dealing with Leonard a good part of the day and now she wasn't sure that she wanted to go out. She had told him she was tired and was going to bed early. She had some sewing she wanted to do. There were a few phone calls she needed to make. Joan was getting spiffed up but Barbara just couldn't seem to get behind it. While she was still sewing, Tom called to see if Joan was ready to go. They were through eating and he and Lyman were ready to move. "Sure," said Joan. Tom and Lyman got into the Buick and cruised over to Barbara Smith's current residence. When they got there, Lyman went up to the house, knocked, and went in. Tom watched the door close from the car. Joan was ready, but Barbara suddenly decided yes, she would go with Joan to the party, if Lyman wouldn't mind waiting a while for her to change her clothes. Lyman didn't mind. Tom didn't know what was happening, but he just sat there at the curb waiting for them all to come out.

Leonard Smith had felt pretty good when he left Barbara

that evening. They'd had two good long talks that day and he could see that they were getting closer. He felt good enough to go out to one of his regular bars, to have a few drinks with people, to feel life getting better for him again. But as time passed, he got to thinking about how good it would be to have Barbara there with him. They could have a few drinks together. It would be like old times. It was really foolish to be out drinking alone when he and his wife were about to get back together. She should be there with him to celebrate. It was about 10:30 when Leonard got back into his car and headed toward Barbara's place on Johnson Street.

Meanwhile, Tom was getting tired of sitting in the car in front of Barbara's house on Johnson. It had been about twenty minutes now and he fidgeted about restlessly in the dark. Then he heard the sounds of familiar voices, looked up, and saw Joan, Barbara, and Lyman coming down the walk toward him. They came up to the car and Joan got into the front seat with him. Lyman opened the back door for Barbara and she moved across the back seat to sit behind Tom. Lyman got in after her. Tom started the car and they headed down toward Fifth Avenue.

Leonard had turned his car into Johnson Street just in time to see Barbara standing beside a car with some man. He pulled his own car to a halt in the middle of the street and watched as the two of them got into the car. What was this guy doing? Whatever he was doing, Leonard knew right away that he didn't have any business doing it with his wife, whoever he was. He couldn't believe Barbara was messing around with someone else right after she'd as good as told him that she'd be coming back to him soon.

As the two got in the car, Leonard continued to watch. The Buick started up, then pulled away from the curb. In a daze, Leonard followed it down Johnson till it turned onto Fifth, a one-way street, then past Harrison, Tyler, and Buchanan. As they were coming up toward Jackson, Leonard pulled his car up along the right side of the Buick. He could see Barbara and this guy laughing and talking in the back seat. The guy leaned forward. Was he kissing her on the cheek? Whispering in her ear? Leonard dropped his car back a little.

Joan and Barbara both saw Leonard at the same time, but neither spoke aloud. Joan formed the words with her mouth, "Did you see that?" Barbara silently acknowledged the sight.

The Buick went through the green light at Jackson and Fifth and Tom heard a sudden noise. He looked out the front window on his right, saw a man in a two-tone car staring in at him, his eyes bugged, and a shotgun barrel pointing toward them. Barbara cried out from the back seat. The two-tone car zipped ahead. Tom looked behind him and saw Lyman slumped over, blood coming out of his head.

"Tom," Barbara called out, "I seen him, I seen him. Go and get him. That's my old stupid husband." But Tom, more concerned with the fate of his bleeding nephew, brushed her comments aside. "I got to get Lyman to the hospital." He stopped the car in the middle of the street, and Tom, Joan, and Barbara got out of the car as a crowd began to gather. Barbara, who was also bleeding from a pellet wound in the back of her head, ran across the street to call for the police and an ambulance. They arrived quickly and Lyman Bostock was rushed off to the hospital where he died within a few hours.

Early the next morning—close to four o'clock—Leonard Smith was awakened by the sound of the doorbell ringing and a scuffling outside his apartment door. He heard his mother asking the police not to hurt him and immediately afterward they were in the room, surrounding him, and he was under arrest.

On September 24 the front page of the *Chicago Tribune* carried the news of Lyman Bostock's death. On September 25 the front page carried the news of Leonard Smith's arrest. There was a picture of Lyman on the front page, looking serious but good-natured with his carefully sculptured mustache and goatee. The third page carried a picture of Leonard, probably taken at the police station when he was being booked, in which he looks startled, dazed, and disheveled.

There was little question that Leonard Smith had done the shooting. Barbara and Joan both recognized him; Tom Turner had picked him out of a lineup, although the identification was very hesitant and unsure. At the trials, Tom couldn't say for a fact that Leonard was the man he had seen staring at him from behind the shotgun barrel. None of the many people milling around the corner of Fifth and Jackson that night had been able to make an identification, but the car descriptions matched. Leonard had a two-tone car just like the one in which everybody reported seeing the killer flee.

The case really looked solid. Surely Leonard would plead guilty to a reduced charge and save everybody the trouble and expense of a trial whose outcome was inevitable. But it didn't turn out that way. The case turned out to have some weaknesses. For example, they couldn't find the shotgun. Leonard had owned a shotgun, Barbara recalled, but Leonard said he'd sold it back in June. In any case, Leonard's shotgun had a regular length barrel, while all the witnesses reported seeing something smaller—a sawed-off shotgun. Barbara didn't recall Leonard ever having one of those, and Leonard denied ever owning one. The police had found Leonard's car parked on a Gary street shortly after the murder. Leonard's wallet was in the car, but there wasn't a shotgun, sawed-off or otherwise.

The absence of the gun and Leonard's denial of owning such a gun was probably more against him than for him. The basic question then became, what was Leonard doing with the gun in the car? What was he planning? If anyone had testified that Leonard tended to travel with a gun regularly, then its use in the "heat of passion," as it were, might be explainable. But if he didn't own such a gun, what was he doing with it in the car that night when he drove back to Barbara's house? Was he planning to ask her out for a drink or was he planning to remove her permanently from his life? The gun became a sticky point in the case.

On the other hand, there was Leonard's contention that he had blacked out events from the time he saw Barbara and the unknown man by the car in front of her house until the next morning when the police woke him in his bed. There was nothing, he claimed, just the sight of his wife and some man and then a blank.

Leonard had no history of blackouts, no evidence of any kind of medical problems that would account for such an event. But he was steadfast in his claim of being able to recall nothing. Of course, it wouldn't be surprising that he might repress the recollection and that such "forgetting" would be the most natural survival action possible. At the trial, the options offered were that he had experienced a mental collapse of some sort, which resulted in a blackout or that he was faking it as a self-serving, calculated means of self-protection. How much simpler an explanation it would be that he unconsciously repressed the memory of this murderous act. Whatever kind of person Leonard was, he was not a casual killer and such an action would have been better forgotten.

But Leonard's attorney thought there was a possibility of an insanity defense. Leonard's apparently genuine inability to remember what had happened was one point. The mental illness in Leonard's family was a second point. Third, there was the obsessional quality of Leonard's views on home and family and the torment Barbara had caused him. It could all add up to a reasonable insanity defense. The lawyer would have to prove mental illness and he would have to prove Leonard's inability to understand the wrongfulness of that act or his inability to control his actions. He thought he could do both.

The court appointed Dr. Hogle, a psychiatrist, to examine Leonard in the county jail beginning in December 1978. Dr. Hogle wasn't sure about Leonard's state of mind.

Leonard insisted he had had a blackout, and certainly the family history was sufficiently problematic, but Hogle couldn't be sure about Leonard's sanity. He conducted seven interviews between December 1978 and March 1979. In addition, he spoke with members of Leonard's family, with a close friend of Leonard's, and with Barbara. At the trial, Dr. Hogle acknowledged that this was considerably more interviewing than he would normally undertake as a forensic psychiatric consultant but that he had done so because he was so uncertain about Leonard's sanity. Finally, he concluded that Leonard was sane. He reported that certain factors led him to the decision: (1) that the loss of memory was suspect, because such a loss is always self-serving; (2) that Leonard repeatedly and adamantly denied having a shotgun in his car when circumstantial evidence made it very probable that he did have one; and (3) that Leonard had no clear history of mental disease.

These became critical factors, overriding the stressful situations that had plagued Leonard's life with Barbara. Dr. Hogle gave Leonard as much as he could in his testimony, but he couldn't give him an insanity defense, as much as Leonard's lawyer tried to help him to do so.

Testifying about his interviews with Dr. Hogle, Leonard had said that during the times they met, "we became very emotional, him and I . . . He told me that he had been married once before and he had three children of his own, and that it would be a great crime to humanity if I was convicted of this crime, and that he would do everything in his power to see that I was innocent."

Dr. Hogle, when questioned about this by Leonard's attorney, had his own problems of recall. He acknowledged that "there were times as I heard him relating his story to me when I felt much sympathy for this man." Q. "Did [this sympathy] result in you also shedding some tears, Doctor, when you talked to him?" A. "Not that I particularly remember. I wouldn't want to say. As I say, I did feel very sympathetic. I don't recall shedding any tears, no."

And did Doctor Hogle really tell Leonard that he should not be convicted of the crime for which he was charged?

"No, sir, I don't recall. I do recall comforting him. I felt that as much as he was hurting . . . he needed some comforting."

Dr. Hogle gave what he could, but it wasn't quite enough. On July 12, 1979, the jury began deliberations. Eight men and two women were convinced of Smith's guilt, but the other two men bought the insanity defense, which resulted in a hung jury.

The second trial began in November of the same year. It was also a relatively short trial. The composition of the jury had changed considerably. This time there were nine women and three men, instead of the ten men and two women in the first trial. There were four blacks this time instead of two. Leonard Smith didn't testify. Everything he had offered into evidence in the previous trial was brought in through questioning other witnesses. The same two court-appointed psychiatrists told their tales, but this time Dr. Hogle was even a little more uncertain about Leonard's mental status, though he still thought he was legally sane. The important new feature at the second trial was Frank Brogno, Ph.D.

Dr. Brogno was a clinical psychologist, a long-time Gary practitioner. He gave Leonard a battery of psychological tests with standardized scoring including tests scored by computer. He testified in a matter-of-fact, down-to-earth manner about his findings without any apparent desire to try to get Leonard off the charge. He explained his findings in a low-key, nontechnical way. Leonard, he said, was a typical schizophrenic personality who could go off at any time. His family history, particularly that of his two sisters, showed evidence of the tendency. If pushed too far, he would be unable to exert proper control.

The prosecution cross-examined Dr. Brogno vigorously, but he remained firm in his opinions. He had tests, he had test scores, he had scientific profiles. It was just a matter of demonstrating psychological facts.

Fourteen months after Lyman Bostock was killed, the Los Angeles Angels finished another season with a new right fielder, Barbara Smith's divorce came through, and Leonard Smith was found not guilty by reason of insanity by a jury of his peers who found the new psychiatric-psychological evidence regarding Leonard Smith's insanity just what they needed to hear. Although Leonard was acquitted of the charges, because the grounds for acquittal were mental illness/insanity, he was sent off for a ninety-day evaluation to see if something needed to be done to correct his mind. The jurors thought their verdict would result in Leonard's spending a long time in a mental hospital, and that Leonard wasn't really all that dangerous if he were to be released someday. He didn't, after all, appear to be a killer at heart. Just a man driven over the edge by a heartless wife.

The *Indiana Star/News* carries the following post-trial chronology of the Lyman Bostock homicide in their library:

Dec. 20, 1979
Leonard Smith, acquitted last month in the slaying of Lyman Bostock, will undergo psychiatric care in the state mental hospital at Logansport.

Mar. 6, 1980
Leonard Smith, accused of the murder of Bostock, will appear in court tomorrow to learn if he will remain in the Logansport State Hospital or be set free.

Mar. 8, 1980
Further mental treatment has been ordered for Leonard Smith, who won an acquittal by reason of insanity in shooting death of Lyman Bostock.

Apr. 9, 1980
Lake County Prosecutor Jack Crawford has asked the judge of Lake County Superior Court to transfer the case of Leonard Smith, acquitted by reason of insanity in the death of Lyman Bostock, to Lake Circuit Judge Felix Kaul who has the authority to keep Smith confined indefinitely under a civil commitment.

June 6, 1980
Doctors no longer consider Leonard Smith insane and have asked a Lake County Judge to order his release from a mental hospital.

June 21, 1980
June 20th, Leonard Smith walked out of a state mental hospital a free man almost seven months after convincing jurors that he was insane when he killed baseball star Lyman Bostock.

Psychiatrists are engaged in what is frequently called a "helping profession," and the thrust of their training is to make them more sensitive helpers. The forensic psychiatrist is, or is supposed to be, a kind of judge, an evaluator of the state of mind of another human being. A clinical psychiatrist, on the other hand, treats people and helps them get better. Both Dr. Hogle and Dr. Brogno wanted to help Leonard Smith, to give him an opportunity to get better. Leonard Smith engaged the sympathy of the forensic psychiatrists and the jury alike. Here was a man whose pain and dreams could touch them, and move them to try to save him. They believed that if he killed Lyman Bostock, it was only by mistake. If he had killed his wife, which may well be what he meant to do, it was only because the agonies he had endured had driven him to do it, past the understanding of right and wrong and past an inability to stop himself from performing such an act. He could do such a thing only if he were crazy, and Dr. Brogno had shown the jurors an objective and apparently scientific guide to Leonard's state of mind, to an assessment of mental illness and lack of capacity, and to a verdict of not responsible by reason of insanity.

For three months after the verdict the psychiatrists evaluated Leonard Smith and for almost four months they treated him. Counting the time he spent in jail before the second trial verdict, Leonard Smith was in prison or in the hospital for only twenty-one months.

The reaction to the verdict led Indiana state legislators to pass a law providing for a verdict of guilty but mentally ill. It might be that under that law, Leonard Smith would still have served only a short period of time, but at least the jury would have had to say that he was guilty.

The first trial was remarkable in that even when no psychiatrist was prepared to say that Leonard Smith met the legal definition of insanity, two jurors were so committed to acquitting him that they were able to deadlock the jury and force a second trial. In that first trial, one psychiatrist was very sympathetic toward Smith, and his testimony, along with the defense lawyer's arguments, may well have been what swayed those two jurors.

That Smith engaged the jury's sympathies is only conjecture as far as the first trial is concerned. In the second trial, the jury made a remarkable turnaround that bears evidence of a deep level of empathy for Smith. The first trial jury was deadlocked, ten to two *for conviction*. The second jury voted twelve to zero for acquittal. The major difference was a single psychologist who testified that Smith was incapable, because of mental illness, of forming the required intent for murder. The jury bought his version of events over that of the prosecution's psychiatrist, but they must have been very anxious to believe what Dr. Brogno asserted. It is true that he presented his opinion in an appealing way and his evidence came dressed in scientific attire, but machine scoring of tests cannot alone account for this dramatic shift in the jury's conclusions about Smith's sanity. The first jury's position suggests the incipient sympathy for Leonard Smith. The second jury's verdict confirms it. But the jurors needed a psychotherapist to authorize their desire not to punish this forlorn man.

It is perhaps true that Leonard Smith poses no further threat to society and cannot benefit from treatment, but this alone does not justify his acquittal for killing Lyman Bostock and his prompt release from the mental hospital, because that could be said of many murderers. This case is a clear miscarriage of justice and abuse of the insanity plea. It was made possible by the attorney who pursued it, the psychotherapists who participated in it, and the jury who bought the sorry bill of goods. The therapist in this case appears to be the primary perpetrator of the outrageous acquittal, but in fact he is merely someone used by the legal system to rationalize and dignify verdicts and sentences that otherwise are not only unjust but unjustifiable.

Some psychiatrists who are competent to do so refuse on principle to testify in any aspect of a criminal trial if their opinion will be used to determine guilt. Many others, however, both competent and incompetent, are more than willing to take on these impossible questions. Those psychiatrists who testify only for the defense or for the prosecution may well be criticized for their motives, but the intentions of those who testify for both sides may be equally suspect: they believe that they can identify mental illness retrospectively and that they can find a causal relationship between the illness and the criminal act. We have no proof that they, or anyone else, can reliably do either of these. We have far more substantial data to suggest that lie detector evidence is accurate and reliable than we have to suggest that psychiatric evidence is accurate, let alone reliable. It is obviously *not* reliable, simply because there is so much disagreement among practitioners. Yet psychiatric evidence is admitted and lie detector evidence is not. Lie detector evidence would have been far more useful in this case than psychiatric evidence, if justice were to be served.

Leonard Smith shot and killed Lyman Bostock. There is no doubt about that. He did not do it in a quiet frame of mind, but few murders are committed in reflective calmness. They are usually the product of anger, jealousy, and fury. That Smith had reached such an emotional state is understandable. He was ill-served in a hard world. But that does not excuse his conduct: it only explains it.

It is surely the case that Smith's mental state influenced his conduct, but that matter should have been weighed when the punishment for the crime was considered—not when guilt was determined. Leonard Smith was guilty and should have been found guilty. He should have received treatment and he should have gone to prison. He should not have been released after seven months. In effect, the criminal justice system told Leonard Smith he could have one almost-free murder to make up for his sad life. That was no bargain—and no justice—for anyone.

TEX WATSON

Battle of the Superstars

THE MONTH OF AUGUST 1969 BROUGHT TWO NIGHTS OF shocking murders to Los Angeles. Just after midnight, on August 9, five people were massacred in the plush Benedict Canyon home of international movie director Roman Polanski. The victims were Sharon Tate, a promising young actress who was Polanski's wife and who was in her eighth month of pregnancy; Jay Sebring, Tate's former boyfriend and a well-known Hollywood hair stylist; Abigail Folger, heiress to the Folger coffee fortune; Voytek Frykowski, a friend of both Miss Folger and Roman Polanski; and Stephen Parent, a teenage acquaintance of the young caretaker who lived in a cottage on the property. The following night, farther east in Los Angeles near Griffith Park, Rosemary and Leo LaBianca suffered the same tragic fate. The killings were nightmarish—multiple stab wounds, a fork left in a body, words carved in flesh, and the victims' blood used to write gibberish messages on walls and doors.

The social chaos of the 1960s had made Los Angeles an

anxious place. Thousands of young people had flocked to the city to participate in the hippy life-style whose visible and audible hallmarks seemed to be unlimited sex, drugs, and rock-'n-roll. The murders appeared to be the dark side of all this sensory abundance.

On December 1, almost three months after the murders, the police department announced that they had solved the "crime of the decade." They charged Charles Manson with plotting the murders and five members of the "Manson family" with the actual killings. Manson was exactly what the public feared in the hippy movement. He was a drifter, a doper, and a dropout—a conscienceless man who had spent most of his life in prison. But he was also a man with a remarkable charismatic quality and, riding the wave of the times, he attracted a band of teenage followers who were prepared to throw over all their traditional values and to adopt Charlie Manson's warped ideas.

The Manson family lived a scrabbly hand-to-mouth existence at a place called the Spahn Ranch, which was occasionally used as a movie location for westerns. What the family had in plenty on the Spahn Ranch were time, isolation, dusty land, drugs, and sex. Manson, like some B-movie Fagin, taught them how to be criminals.

The family members who took part in the murders were Linda Kasabian, Susan Atkins, Leslie Van Houten, Patricia Krenwinkel, and Charles "Tex" Watson, young people from ordinary middle-class American homes. Linda Kasabian turned state's evidence and was given judicial immunity in return for her testimony against the others. Manson, Atkins, Van Houten, and Krenwinkel were tried together in a veritable circus of a trial that resulted in their receiving guilty verdicts and death sentences. The death sentences were later overturned by the U.S. Supreme Court in a general ruling that struck down the death penalty statute as unconstitutional.

Tex Watson fled to Texas in November 1969, and was not returned to California because of extradition problems for many months. As a result, Watson was tried alone, after Manson and his girls had been tried, found guilty, and sentenced.

The stories of the murders gave sufficient detail to suggest that, if any murder could be characterized as an act of insanity, then surely these could: the "helter skelter" writings in blood on the walls and furniture, plus the fact that the victims had been stabbed repeatedly, even long after they were dead. Yet, at the conclusion of the trials of Manson, Atkins, Van Houten, Krenwinkle, and Tex Watson, the juries returned verdicts containing not even the slightest suggestion that they thought these murderers were insane, that they had acted under the influence of intoxicating drugs, or, indeed, had acted under diminished capacity of any sort. All the defendants were found guilty—fully and totally responsible for their actions.

The verdicts were not really a surprise. But there is something puzzling about them if we recall that the 1960s were a time when the fear of drug use was of intense concern to most parents. Every day, in conversation, in newspapers, in magazines, and on television, we heard repeated tales of the manifest dangers and prevalence of illegal drugs. The air was filled with stories of young people on drugs and the craziness that enveloped them and their lives: a twenty-year-old on LSD who walked out of a fifteenth-story window convinced that he could fly; multiple auto crashes on freeways caused by doped-up teeny-boppers who later reported from hospital beds that it "had been like driving a gazelle!"; and sexual orgies in public or near public that no sane person could imagine taking part in or even wanting to take part in. In 1969 this country had every reason to believe that too many drugs—and especially such hallucinogens as LSD, mescaline, psilocybin, and marijuana—destroyed the mind. The country genuinely feared for its children. But when a vast amount of drug use was reported in the Manson and Watson trials, the jury forgot that drugs made you crazy and did not for a second believe that drug craziness was a defense.

No one ever doubted that Charlie Manson and his playmates had too many drugs. There was plenty of evidence of that. The array of psychiatric stars who analyzed the origins of the crime-of-the-decade testified about the abundance of drugs and had heard about the Manson life-style and the Manson murders from the lips of those who belonged to the family. Predictably, the psychiatrists who testified for the defense thought the murderers were crazy, so far beyond their senses as to not be responsible in any meaningful way for what they did. The psychiatrists who testified for the prosecution found the Manson group fully capable, despite their life-style, of knowing right from wrong and acting upon that knowledge. The jury had to make some sense both of the murders and murderers, but how was it possible to understand something so horrendous? The choices seemed limited: either these young people *were* crazy (good children from good homes whose lives had been corrupted and minds destroyed by drugs), or they were monsters (sexually perverse exhibitionists, drug addicts, dirty hippies, criminals), and not at all like other people. One psychiatrist offered yet another view: they were prodigal sons and daughters who had given up the struggle of life for the pleasures of the flesh (a somewhat less than comprehensive explanation).

Perhaps as individuals and as judges, in the sense that jurors are judges, we are least able to tolerate the gratuitous murder: the murder of absolute strangers for which there is no explanation or justification—not money, revenge, anger, or even deluded self-protection. These are the murders that are most threatening to us because we cannot protect ourselves from them; they are the genuinely and thoroughly irrational murders. There are other murders that we abhor but find less fearsome, such as the young mother without friends or money who murders a child because of her desperate inability to care for it, and we recognize (though we should not forgive) the despair and anxiety.

In the Manson case, however, there was no such recognition of despair or anxiety. These wayward souls had not painted themselves into a corner from which blind vision forced a murderous exit. Instead, they committed acts of total irrationality—and, the jury declared, of total sanity. How the crime could be totally irrational and the criminals totally rational is not clear. This is one of the glaring paradoxes of the criminal justice system, but one not infrequently seen, as for example, New York's Son of Sam, L.A.'s Hillside Strangler and Freeway Killer, and San Francisco's Zodiac Killer. Perpetrators of multiple murders who act out crazy scenarios are seldom found not guilty by reason of insanity. Most frequently, they plead guilty to a reduced charge or to a promise of a life imprisonment instead of a death sentence. The Manson trials were unusual in that respect simply because such cases do not often go to trial. But when they do, they provide an exceptionally clear view of the psychiatric expert witness, his skills, his role, and the multiple possibilities in and of his judgments.

Manson, Atkins, Van Houten, and Krenwinkle were tried together in 1970. Tex Watson, alleged to have done most of the actual killing, was tried separately in 1971, after the Manson trial, because of the extradition problems resulting from Watson's flight to Texas. In his lengthy trial, nine psychiatrists and one psychologist testified. Some were appointed by the court and others were selected by the prosecution and by the defense.

It is difficult to imagine a trial in which ten ballistics experts or ten fingerprint identification experts would be called. In general, an expert witness is someone who interprets technical information of a more or less quantifiable nature. Although experts might disagree about the statistical degree of accuracy of the tests they perform, it is unusual to find expert witnesses in full disagreement with one another about whether, say, the blood stains or fingerprints match those of the accused (or the victim). Technical expert witnesses generally work from some kind of common view about their area of expertise—i.e., they all perform the same tests in the same way; and their skill is in reading the results, not in creating the tests, in deciding which ones to administer, or simply deciding to do some interesting things when they have no standard tests. Where there are no standard tests, most experts would say that they cannot provide information. Usually, if experts are equally experienced and competent, their readings or interpretations will be consistent because they share the same assumptions and methods. They may disagree about the firmness of their conclusions, but not about the conclusions themselves. This is not, however, true of expert psychiatric testimony. Psychotherapeutic expert witnesses are members of a profession that has no generally agreed upon, scientifically based standard of knowledge with respect to the issues of insanity and legal responsibility. As a result, one can scarcely compare the assessment of one psychiatrist to another, so different are their methods and purposes.

The ten expert psychiatric witnesses in Tex Watson's trial all presented different views of Watson's mind and of his guilt. By analyzing the testimony of four of them (two for the prosecution and two for the defense), it is possible to see an interesting array of psychiatric testimony and to imagine how difficult it was for the jury to listen to Drs. K. Grovner Bailey, Joel Fort, Keith Ditman, and Richard Walter, and to draw from their very different conclusions any guidance about the state of Tex Watson's mind on those murderous evenings in 1969. The judge, in a conference at the bench during the trial, away from the jury's hearing, expressed his frustration with the psychiatric testimony quite succinctly: "All this psychiatric testimony leaves me cold. To me it is a lot of gobbledegook and double talk. . . . I wish we could get along without it, but I guess we can't."

The jury had no opportunity to go on record with their opinions of psychiatric testimony and to what use they put it. At times it must have seemed to them that the only advantage these doctors had over the jurors themselves was that the psychiatrists had talked to Tex prior to the trial and had asked their own questions. But, in most instances, they had interviewed Tex only weeks or days before the trial, two years after the crimes, and they seemed to have asked Tex the same questions asked by the lawyers, so perhaps even the psychiatrists had little advantage. Since the jurors had heard Tex testify, they could at least compare their own conclusions with the experts' judgments about whether or not anyone could believe what Tex said. Some of the experts did believe him; some of them didn't.

In a California homicide trial, expert psychiatric testimony goes ultimately to three legal questions:

1. Did the defendant at the time of the crime have the mental capacity to harbor malice aforethought?
2. Did the defendant at the time of the crime have the mental capacity to maturely and meaningfully reflect upon the gravity of the contemplated act of killing?
3. Did the defendant at the time of the killing have the mental capacity to deliberate and premeditate the killings?

These are the only questions relevant to psychiatric expertise. It is important to note that the court does not require the expert witness to state whether the defendant did in fact harbor malice, reflect maturely and meaningfully upon the gravity of his act, or deliberate and premeditate the killings, although the experts regularly answered that question as well, until the law was changed in 1982. Many argue that these are questions of fact and thus more appropriately to be decided by the jury, not testified to by psychiatrists. The psychiatric expert does testify about the defendant's capacity or ability to form and understand criminal intent: i.e., could he have done A, B, or C if he had wanted to or had chosen to. This distinction—between *could* he and *did* he—presumably separates the expert's conclusion from the jury's deliberations. Expert testimony would, in theory, totally override the jury's deliberations only if every psychiatric witness testified that the defendant had no capacity for the three relevant factors. If all the experts agreed that the defendant was incapable of forming criminal intent, the jury would have difficulty finding that he acted criminally since he lacked the ability to act criminally. Expertise carries at least that much weight, but these psychiatric opinions are so speculative about capacity that there is always a divergence of opinion. It is probable that there would be a difference of opinion even if the three factors were defined in some specific way. Since they are not (the description above is about as specific as the law gets), almost any behavior can be interpreted as evidence for or against capacity.

Another reason for this divergence in psychiatric testimony and conclusions is that the witnesses are required to testify about the defendant's capacity at the time of the alleged criminal act. They have difficulty agreeing about the defendant's capacity at the time of examination, even if they all examined him at the same time. When the examinations are all at different times and are conducted months or even years after the crime (as they were with Tex Watson), it is hard to imagine what they would assess or how they would do it. The expert witnesses in this case acknowledged the difficulty of performing such after-the-fact assessments. They approached the difficult task by circling about, speculating, offering generalities, and finally trying, in most instances, to base their judgments on two conditions: the probable presence of psychosis and the probable presence of brain damage. (Even on these points, the witnesses differed in their judgment of the relative importance of the two conditions, as well as their definitions of them.) Dr. Bailey maintained that his examination showed that Tex Watson had been and continued to be psychotic but had no brain damage; Dr. Walter had no opinion about psychosis but believed Watson to have brain damage; Dr. Fort argued that Watson was neither psychotic nor brain damaged; Dr. Ditman asserted that Watson was both psychotic and brain damaged. The interesting result of these various assessments was that Dr. Bailey and Dr. Fort, who disagreed about Watson's psychotic state but agreed there was no brain damage, found Watson to have the capacity necessary for criminal responsibility; and Dr. Ditman and Dr. Walter, who agreed there was brain damage but disagreed about the psychosis, believed Watson did not possess the requisite capacity for criminal responsibility. Lest the brain-damage assessment be considered the focal point, it should be noted that Dr. Bailey agreed that Dr. Walter's assessment of brain damage was probably correct but that he didn't observe damage in *his* tests, conducted at a different time. Neither of them, however, conducted their tests even remotely near the time of the murders.

Dr. Bailey was appointed by the judge and testified for the prosecution in *People* v. *Watson*. Bailey, a veteran of thirty-five years of participation in criminal evaluations and a former professor at the California College of Medicine and Chief of the Neurosurgery Ward at County General Hospital, was in his seventies at the time of the trial and was often a rambling witness. He could effortlessly fall into a long digression about a recent James Michener novel, using it as an example of the kind of problem he thought society was facing and that Charlie Manson exemplified. But if he was at times a garrulous old man reminiscing about the 5,000 criminal cases in which he had been asked to examine defendants, he was also the beloved Dr. Welby who worried about Tex Watson's eating habits as much as about his mental state, even if he was a mass murderer. In many respects, Bailey's great success as an expert witness for the prosecution was that he never failed to convey his sense of Watson as a fellow human being. It was as if he testified not as a technical expert but as a beloved and loving sage, speaking from his heart, saying that he had come to know this young man closely, better in fact than Tex knew himself, and that with the closeness of this human understanding came the sad knowledge that Tex knew what he was doing and thus should be held fully accountable. If a man like Dr. Bailey who cared about Tex was forced to come to that conclusion, what could a poor juror do?

Bailey spent about eight hours examining Watson over a period of about two weeks. He devoted a longer period of time to the examinations than did most of the other expert witnesses, who were participating only on a consultant basis. The way the time was spent also differed significantly. Bailey conducted a physical examination (the only one of the doctors to do so), gave a series of informal verbal tests and paper and pencil tests, inquired about the past and the present, and discussed Tex's eating problems and room arrangements (eventually managing to get Tex a room to himself and hospital/infirmary food that Tex was better able to eat). Dr. Bailey definitely was not all psychiatric business. Instead, he was all human—his concern, genuine; his psychiatric tests, vague.

He had Tex do the Draw-a-Person test; his interpretive conclusion was that if Tex had drawn the figure in the lower half of the page, it would have indicated some organic damage, such as brain damage. However, Tex drew it in the upper left-hand corner, which meant that Tex felt himself cornered (the jury might have guessed he felt that way without any fancy tests). Although the Draw-a-Person test is one widely used by psychotherapists of all persuasions and has some generally agreed upon interpretations, Bailey's description of it made it sound about as accurate as reading tea leaves. He showed a few Rorschach test cards to Tex, the Rorschach being a widely used, respected, and, to some degree, standardized test in which subjects are asked to describe what a series of ink blots reminds them of. Bailey checked to see if Tex saw the same things in each of them. When he did not, Bailey noted this as evidence of no brain damage, since brain-damaged people often get "stuck in a groove," as he phrased it, seeing the same figure in each card. But Bailey did not actually conduct a complete Rorschach test. As an expert witness, he seemed anything but technically expert. At one point, he commented, almost as an aside, that he had great reservations about his own testimony, a statement of doubt so unexpected from an expert witness that the defense lawyer responded, querulously, "Surely you are amusing us with that statement?"

The district attorney who prosecuted the case against Tex Watson said to the judge that "the heart of this whole trial is the psychiatric testimony." He was right, for there was no disputing the facts: there were seven grisly murders and Watson's hand had surely been on the knife and the gun. Manson, Krenwinkel, Van Houten, and Atkins had already been found guilty.

Dr. Bailey had read all the testimony from their trial and all the other psychiatric reports. He had, he reported, spent over 300 hours on the Watson case and had prepared a fifty-four page report based on over 200 pages of notes. It seemed that, in the two or three months since he had become involved in the case, he had devoted his every working hour to the assessment of Tex Watson. When he finally presented his conclusions to the jury, they were judgments not only of Watson's capacity. Under cross-examination, Bailey enigmatically stated that although Tex Watson did not know why he committed the murders, Bailey himself did. The defense attorney wisely avoided asking any further questions along this line, but when the district attorney returned to ask his final questions, he did ask Bailey to reveal why Tex had done it.

Watson, according to Bailey, was psychotic. He had a kind of unusual psychosis called *folie-à-deux*, in which he joined with Manson in believing in an unreal version of reality. He wanted a stronger person to make his decisions for him, to sweep him along in the world, and to give life meaning. Manson was charistmatic, powerful, and had a set of beliefs; Watson was weak, empty, and an immature follower.

Together they formed a unit and made a contract: Manson made decisions and interpreted reality and, in exchange, Tex was given a life without inhibitions, one in which he could have all his wants satisfied, particularly his sexual ones. Manson would provide; Watson would obey. But, Bailey argued, this was no loss of competence. It was a voluntary, willing surrender. Watson was "enjoying the indulgences and satiety of the 'family' life at the ranch and, paying a price as a wastrel far exceeding the 'riotous living' of the prodigal son, is now, as that prototype did, and as the defendant himself told me, 'asking for forgiveness' and desperately desiring to return to his father's home." Tex had, Bailey continued, "played the game, learned the rules, abided by the rules, obeyed the coach." The inevitable conclusion to Bailey's analysis was that Tex had succumbed to his own human weakness, the character flaws that are potential in everyone, and that his sin, unlike the prodigal son's, could not merely be forgiven. Tex must pay for his actions, must be held accountable and responsible.

Dr. Bailey often cloaked his testimony in almost incomprehensible language (his first definition of *folie-à-deux* was: "a psychosis simultaneously involving two or more intimately related persons, relationships, both biological and environmental, a psychiatric entity characterized by transference of delusional ideas and/or abnormal behavior from one person to one or more others who have been in close association with the primarily affected patient." Although this testimony contained some scientific or technical information, Bailey basically presented a profoundly *moral* judgment, not a scientific assessment, of the events that led to the murders and of Tex Watson's involvement in them. He gave the jury a set of reasons and motivations that they could understand and that they could use to support a guilty verdict. They knew Tex Watson was not like them, for nothing but total craziness could account for such actions in people like them. But Tex did share something with them, Bailey told them: the desire to give in, to satisfy every desire whenever you want to, to let someone else make all the hard decisions. The jury could imagine such a desire—but they knew deep within their being that giving into easy pleasures and satisfactions and giving up the challenge of life are morally wrong and must be punished.

Dr. Bailey explained throughout his 220 pages of testimony that Tex did not lack capacity—he was simply weak. He never explained how these two differ or how the difference could be determined. If Bailey's "expertise" rings true, if his conclusions sound right, it is because he touches an intuitive response in us, not because he has made a sound or convincing logical, technical, or psychiatric argument.

Dr. Joel Fort also testified as a witness for the prosecution and claimed that Tex Watson was neither psychotic nor brain damaged. Watson, in his estimation, had the capacity when the murders were committed two years earlier, to harbor malice aforethought, to maturely and meaningfully reflect upon the gravity of the contemplated act, and to deliberate and premeditate the acts of murder with which he was charged.

Like Dr. Bailey, Fort was appointed by the judge in the case to interview and evaluate Tex Watson. Fort had extensive experience and was well known to the public as an expert in the area of drug use and abuse. He was the founder of the San Francisco City Drug Program, the first such program in the country to deal with the drug abuse phenomenon of the 1960s. In the halcyon days of Haight-Ashbury, Fort frequently appeared on serious talk shows, spoke authoritatively at legislative hearings, and consulted for international organizations and foreign countries. In the criminal justice system he was noted for his frequent appearances, including testimony in two of Timothy Leary's trials and at one of Lenny Bruce's trials.

Dr. Fort's academic credentials and public service were impressive. He was running Fort Help, a big clinic in San Francisco, and in connection with that and other clinics and hospitals, he acknowledged that he had been directly involved in the psychiatric treatment of drug abusers and had personally seen more than 10,000 of them. If anyone could make sense of the countercultural, drug-filled, rebellious life-style of Charlie Manson and his associates, Dr. Fort surely could. He had some expertise in the Manson murder trials as well, since he had testified on behalf of Leslie Van Houten in the penalty phase of her trial.

Fort saw himself as an impartial witness who could only bring technical, "neutral" information to the jury. When asked about his testimony for the defense in the previous trial, he responded that he did not like to think of himself as testifying for the defense. In fact, he suggested, he simply brought such information as he had drawn from his interview with Tex Watson to the jury for their aid. The inference was that he came only to bring facts that the jury needed to know and that they were in no position to find out.

Unlike Dr. Bailey's hourly, day-after-day meetings, Fort met with Watson only once, took twelve to fifteen pages of notes, submitted only a brief report to the judge. He performed no psychological tests. One of the ongoing arguments among the expert witnesses had to do with Watson's intelligence. Watson had performed very poorly on a standard IQ test given to him by a defense witness, Dr. Palmer. The low score he received was significantly contradicted by reports of Watson's intelligence as a high school and college student. There was some suggestion by some of the psychiatrists that this alleged drop in IQ score was further evidence of brain damage caused by the multiple drugs that Watson took regularly (primarily LSD, belladonna, amphetamines, and marijuana). Dr. Bailey had found Watson's intelligence "flawed," an evaluation resulting from Tex's complete inability to explain the meaning of a proverb: "If you make yourself into honey, flies will eat you." Dr. Fort, on the other hand, found him "of above average intelligence," an assessment apparently based on nothing more than that he seemed "pretty intelligent" while they were talking. It is an interesting aspect of expert psychiatric testimony that even when there is objective information available (such as standard IQ tests), the experts are encouraged to give opinions without the benefit of such tests. It is hard to imagine that either Bailey's or Fort's opinions about Watson's intelligence were of greater credibility than the opinion of the average person.

Like Bailey, Fort found Tex to be a weak person who was greatly attracted to and under the influence of Charles Manson. He thought this weakness was the source of Watson's participation in the murders. He did not, however, find this character weakness to be either pathologic or psychotic. When asked on what he based his judgment, Fort replied:

"On the material [Tex] presented to me about his state of mind, his thinking, his actions at that time, and also the material in the transcripts and depositions . . . neither of those things indicates that he was showing any signs of hallucinations, delusions, any kind of symptoms or mental change that would impair his capacity to form an intent or premeditate or deliberate."

Fort testified with precision, crispness, and clarity (or at least the illusion of it). His answers seem certain and, unlike Dr. Bailey, it is doubtful that he had any reservations about his testimony. When asked if he had an opinion, he replied, "Yes, I have an opinion on that," and then waited to be asked his opinion. But the crispness and certainty of his answers seem superficial when examined closely. When asked, for example, about his opinion of whether LSD users are in contact with reality and recognize that the unusual effects they are experiencing are the product of the drug he replied, "The usual user or taker of those drugs is in contact with reality." But in a full page of amplification of this response, there is never a hint of how this truth might apply to Tex Watson, who could scarcely be described as "the usual user or taker."

Fort did not give any hints as to how the jury was to take this solid information he was providing them from his expertise. If Tex was the usual user, then he wouldn't have been driven out of contact with reality by the alleged heavy drug use. But the question was whether Tex *was* "the usual user," that is, whether he *was* normal. As a result, Fort's expertise amounted to something like, "If Tex is normal, he was normal," which was scarcely helpful, but Fort's presentation "sounded" helpful and full of hard information. For example, he distinguished long-term and short-term effects of drug use as follows:

> Well, the differentiation [between short-term and long-term effect] is between what happens with the average dose of the drug on one occasion, within the two to four-hour period or with some drugs, longer period of time that the drug is exerting some influence on the person, or is altering their consciousness in some way; and the long-term effect would be what happens to you psychologically, physically, socially, from chronic use; which, in turn, has to be subdivided into chronic light or moderate use versus chronic heavy or excessive use of the drugs, and you get different pictures or different answers depending upon which of these dimensions you are dealing with.

Later in his testimony Fort indicated that he believed Watson was not under the influence of drugs at the time of the murders, so it is difficult to understand the relevance of all this information about drug use.

Fort found the strongest evidence for Watson's not being psychotic at the time of the murders in the fact that he drove the car, concealed weapons, changed clothes, cut phone wires, killed people, washed blood off himself, and wiped fingerprints off knives. Again, it is difficult to see how this judgment offers technical or expert assistance to the jury. At this point in his testimony Fort, like Bailey, seemed simply to be telling the jury whether he thought Watson ought to be found guilty.

The major thrust of Fort's testimony had to do with the various effects of drugs. As noted earlier, his information was almost always couched in terms of the effects of drugs on the average user. Although no other expert witness had the public reputation for knowledge about drugs that Fort did, the lawyers managed to create an ongoing disagreement about whether heavy use of hallucinogenic and other dangerous drugs could cause brain damage. Dr. Walter maintained that LSD probably caused brain damage, but from a neurological point of view, the evidence went both ways. He also believed that research evidence definitely had connected amphetamine use to organic brain damage and thus believed that Watson's brain damage could be caused by drug use. Dr. Ditman felt that the tests on animals were sufficiently convincing that one could assume brain damage from drug use was possible. Dr. Fort, when asked if he knew of any reported case of brain damage directly attributed to the use of hallucinogens, replied "No. Brain damage does not occur from their use. When damage occurs, it is of a psychological or sometimes social nature, but there is no brain damage in their use."

Given this diversity of psychiatrist opinions, the jury was back to where they had started. They might well feel that they were free to pick and choose among these opinions, the only constraint being that the opinion should match the conclusion they wished to draw about the effect of Watson's drug use on his life and their judgment about him.

The peculiar final feature of Fort's testimony was that he believed Watson was fully responsible for his criminal acts and that Leslie Van Houten had not been fully responsible for hers. His explanation of this difference in his judgment of responsibility stemmed, he explained, from the fact that the women in the Manson family "played a strictly subservient and inferior role, and a woman, therefore, and specifically Leslie, would have been more dominated." It may well be one of the few times that the domination of women by men could have been of potential value to the woman.

Dr. Keith Ditman, a psychiatrist and psychiatric researcher from UCLA, appeared as a witness for the defense.

Unlike Drs. Fort and Bailey, he was not appointed by the judge but was asked to examine Watson by Watson's lawyer. Like Fort, he testified, in part, as an expert in matters of drug use and abuse, but his expertise was more research oriented than clinically oriented, since he had only dealt with hundreds of drug abusers while Fort claimed experience with thousands. In addition, Dr. Ditman testified in the broader areas, specifically on psychosis and brain damage.

He examined Tex on two occasions, both times only a few weeks before the trial and more than two years after the crimes. Prior to examining Watson he had read the reports of eight other experts and the testimony of Linda Kasabian. He also had other background information on the case as a result of his having testified as a witness for the defense at the Manson trial on behalf of Leslie Van Houten.

Ditman's testimony about drug abuse and drug abusers may have been confusing to the jury when they compared it to the testimony given by Dr. Fort. Those who are familiar with psychiatric theory know that there is great disagreement among practitioners even about the accuracy of such aspects as diagnosis, and about the definitions of psychosis. However, they might expect drug experts to be on surer, more scientific grounds. But any such hope was not borne out in the testimony of these two experts.

Did LSD and other hallucinogenic drugs change people? Ditman said yes, while Fort said no. Could these drugs cause you to black out? Fort said no, while Ditman said yes.

Would you, if you had taken belladonna, speed, LSD, and marijuana all at one time, behave in such a way that everyone would know that you were under the heavy influence of drugs? Probably yes, was Fort's answer; not necessarily, said Ditman.

Was Watson psychotic as a result of drug use at the time of the murders? Yes, from Ditman, and no, from Fort.

Do hallucinogenic drugs cause brain damage? Fort stated never, but Ditman said yes.

Did Watson have brain damage? "No," said Fort; "yes," said Ditman.

What could a jury do with such evidence but either believe whichever witness personally appealed to them or discard both opinions?

It is difficult to imagine that the two men could both be considered experts in the same field unless one looks carefully below the surface of their answers for other factors that help to explain the difference. A psychiatrist may be asked to interview and evaluate a defendant by the court, the defense lawyer, or the prosecution lawyer. He will submit a written report if the evaluation is requested by the court. Otherwise, the report may be either written or oral. Having asked the psychiatrist to conduct an evaluation does not oblige the attorney to use the psychiatrist as an expert witness. His testimony would be requested only if the lawyer thought it would be useful to his case. This adversary aspect of criminal trials accounts for some of the disparity in evidence given by expert psychiatric witnesses. In the case of Drs. Fort and Ditman, their answers often were diametrically opposed, but frequently this was a result of the different ways that the attorneys asked questions. For example, throughout the questioning of Dr. Fort about the effects of drugs, questions were posed and answers were given about the ordinary or average user of drugs. With Dr. Ditman, the questions and answers focused on the range of users. Although the questions were not framed in such an obvious way, a comparable pair of questions and answers would be:

1. Do most people who have taken heavy doses of hallucinogens perform complex tasks like climbing telephone poles and breaking into houses? The answer is *no* (both Fort and Ditman would probably agree to that).

2. Is it possible that a person who had taken a heavy dose of hallucinogens could perform complex tasks like climbing telephone poles and breaking into houses? The

answer is *yes*—and, again, both Fort and Ditman would probably agree. But Fort would be asked the first question, and Ditman the second.

The shaping of the testimony by the lawyers is certainly one aspect of psychiatric expert testimony that can be legitimately criticized. Given that psychiatry is an area of study whose contours and contents have not yet been precisely described, the addition of further confusion by lawyers can scarcely be helpful, but it is not the psychiatrists who are to blame (unless it is for being willing to go into the courts at all), for they must answer the questions as they are given. A psychiatric expert witness might be considered accountable for this distortion when he answers questions in such a way as to provide maximum justification for his final conclusions. Thus Fort, who believed that Watson was criminally responsible, always gave answers to questions that provided maximum support for his position, never qualifying his answer if it would not support the prosecution's position. The same charge could be levied at Dr. Ditman.

On the topic of brain damage, Ditman was persuaded by the test results, which were never specified other than "slowness," "hesitancy," and "groping for certain recollections" during the interview, and the EEG performed by Dr. Walter. (Dr. Walter's EEG was a welcome piece of information that all the expert witnesses could speak on. It must have been a relief, as well, to the judge and jury, for it was a tangible record produced by an impartial machine that provided quantifiable results. Unfortunately, there was another EEG given earlier with different results so the impact of this tangibility and precision was lost.) But Ditman's belief in brain damage came from his conviction that anybody who chewed, swallowed, inhaled, and shot up as many street drugs as Tex Watson had, had to be organically affected by the experience. Unlike Fort, who asserted without condition that drug use did not affect the brain in any permanent, harmful way,

Ditman believed that the apparent lack of evidence of brain damage was a result of scientists' inability yet to find it in humans. He referred to animal studies in which brain biopsies showed organic changes after drug ingestion and pointed out, reasonably enough, that comparable studies could scarcely be carried out on humans. But, he argued, human behavior shows that the states of the brain, mind, and body are not disconnected, and "there are psychological indications of brain damage on psychological tests, on neurological tests."

The disagreement in this instance between Fort and Ditman is not one of how questions are asked by lawyers. Rather it is an absolute difference in assumptions or in basic beliefs about human functioning. Fort did not, as did Dr. Walter, say that there is no definitive evidence of drugs causing brain damage, so one could not say for sure whether they do or do not (which would have probably been the most accurate statement—though not very useful to either lawyer if the presence or absence of brain damage was what they wanted to prove). Instead Fort declared that it simply did not happen. Ditman argued that although there was no hard evidence that drugs caused brain damage, they surely must. Such judgments, though made by respected and well-educated men, scarcely qualify as expertise. They are less medical opinion than they are philosophical speculation.

On the question of psychosis Ditman was able to find several possibilities. Upon first interviewing Watson, he thought him to be schizophrenic. He later changed his diagnosis and decided, like Dr. Bailey, that Tex was engaged with Manson in a psychotic *folie-à-deux*, in which Manson provided the paranoid schizophrenia to the partnership. Ditman believed Watson's psychosis was caused by Manson, drugs, and Watson's weak personality, and was manifested by his delusions and hallucinations and the very fact that he performed these gruesome murders. When Ditman tried to explain this belief, the district attorney goaded him repeatedly, finally accusing him of, perhaps, the greatest sin for an expert witness. "Doctor," he said, "in all deference to you and your profession, isn't it true that your testimony about these things is pure unadulterated guess work; isn't that true, Doctor?"

Dr. Ditman's reply suggests the depths of his sincerity and his belief that he had to provide cogent explanations of human behavior that is beyond our understanding. "It has to make some sense, fit together," he answered. "There has to be some explanation for his, for example, behavior when I saw him, how his personality would fit into that setting."

It was as if he were saying "Tex seemed like a human being to me when I interviewed him. If he did those inhuman things, then at that time, he *must* have been crazy."

Dr. Richard Walter was a professor of neurology at the UCLA Neuropsychiatric Institute. His connection with the case was more distant than that of any of the other psychiatrists. Dr. Frank and Dr. Suarez (both psychiatrists who participated in evaluations of Watson) had asked Dr. Walter to perform a neurological exam of Tex as part of their overall evaluation. Alone among the experts, Walter had received no information from Tex Watson about the activities at the Tate or LaBianca residences. He examined Tex in April 1971, approximately four and a half months before the trial began. He had no involvement in the Manson trial and, although he was a highly respected and experienced researcher and teacher, he had testified in only three previous cases and had never before examined a defendant accused of murder.

Dr. Walter personally conducted three series of tests on Tex Watson and interpreted an electroencephalogram (EEG). The tests were for motor function, sensation, and mental status. The EEG was given by Walter's associate to determine whether there were any irregularities or abnormalities in Watson's brain wave activity.

The motor function tests were standard tests checking out each cranial nerve's functioning: how quickly could Watson stick his tongue out repeatedly and how fast could he tap his thumb and index finger together? Could he, while standing on one foot, perform specific activities without losing his balance? Could he touch the doctor's finger, then his own nose? Could he do this if the doctor's finger moved? Walter described a series of simple physical tests that were precise and understandable. His conclusions from the test were equally clear and precise and open to little argument from the attorneys. Walter testified that Watson performed the tests more slowly than did the average subject and frequently had difficulty understanding what he was supposed to do. The sensation tests, on the other hand, were successfully passed by Tex. He was able to hear, see, and touch within an ordinary response range.

When Dr. Walter described the mental status exam that he had administered, he pointed out to the court that he did not use standardized tests but only rule-of-thumb tests. He explained that psychologists were able to give very specific tests in this area and, therefore, there was no need for him to repeat such tests when, for his purposes, he needed only a general sense of mental status. His "rule of thumb" tests were similar to those described by several of the other psychiatrists, but Walter placed them in context with this explanation and made them sound reasonable and productive.

He described Tex's unsuccessful attempts to repeat a semi-nonsense phrase; his weak ability to repeat more than the general outline of a one-paragraph story three minutes after he had heard it; his ability to think of only one thing that apples and oranges have in common (Tex answered that they were both fruits and one was red and the other orange); his inability to repeatedly subtract 7 from 100 (i.e., 100—7=93; 93—7=86; 86—7=79, etc.). He concluded from these tests that Tex's responses were abnormal in several areas.

His final test was the EEG, a machine-made, graphlike tracing of a subject's brain wave activity. This is a highly standardized test and an experienced reader (which Walter was) could tell when a patient blinked his eye, when he fell asleep, even when he began to dream, from patterns of the record. In the case of Watson's brain wave tracing, Walter concluded that the brain wave activity was consistently abnormal and that it demonstrated "classical evidence of brain damage."

Walter was more fortunate than most of the other psychiatric witnesses because his area of expertise permitted him to speak, at least in a limited way, about numbers, averages, and concrete, countable responses. For example, Watson could stick his tongue out only three times per interval whereas the average was eight. As a result, Dr. Walter's testimony appeared to be less a matter of arbitrary opinion.

But his testimony was also sharply differentiated from the other psychiatrists in two other, perhaps more important ways. First, he made minimal claims for his knowledge, always explaining his responses as narrowly as possible and quite candidly saying "I don't know" to questions that required speculative replies. Second, he exhibited no interest whatever in Tex Watson as a person, patient, and murderer. Tex was merely a human organism he had tested, and Walter clearly believed that his expertise did not begin to cover anything as complex as a whole person and his motives.

The carefulness of Dr. Walter's opinion was demonstrated throughout his testimony. When he made clear that his mental status tests were only rough measures, he made it impossible for the prosecution to argue with their precise accuracy. When he was asked how long a period of time Watson had suffered from brain damage, he emphasized that he was only able to get a "feel" for "approximate duration in which this process was going on," thus eliminating any arguments about unjustified and unjustifiable precision. When asked if he had any idea what Watson's brain condition was on the night of the murder, he simply replied no, that he had no idea, instead of making speculative replies about what he thought it might have been given all of the imponderable variables.

Walter was a model of what any expert witness in this field could be if he had no investment in the outcome of events and did not feel that his area of expertise was all of human behavior. The prosecution attorney, in particular, attempted to bait Walter and draw him into making wider, more general claims for his opinion, but Walter repeatedly walked through the fire unscathed. He was firmly and comfortably aware of what he did and did not know.

At one point in the trial, Walter was given the pair of wire cutters that Watson was alleged to have used to cut the telephone wires outside Sharon Tate's house. The cutters were heavy—about fifteen pounds—and Walter was asked if in his opinion Tex Watson could have climbed the pole carrying the cutters, balanced himself at the top of the pole, and cut the four wires if he had had the same motor abilities as Walter had observed in his test. It is a standard hypothetical question that all the psychiatric witnesses were given: could Tex have done X on the night of the murders if he were as (drugged, psychotic, confused, weak, whatever) as you say he was?

There is little doubt from the transcript that every other expert witness would have answered the question in whatever way would have supported their general view of Tex's guilt. Thus, if they thought he was responsible, they would have said "Sure, he could have climbed that pole." If they thought he was not, they might have had doubts about whether he could really have climbed that pole. Walter's initial effort to answer this hypothetical question is superb in its unstudied disclaimer of having much value as an answer: "You must realize that this information is a hunch. I have not put this to the test. It is based in part on the difficulty of trying to decide how much effort is involved in climbing a telephone pole carrying [the wire clippers] and balancing yourself, and that information I don't have."

The attorney interrupted this reply to ask if Walter had in fact ever climbed a telephone pole, to which he said no. After another half-dozen attempts to get Walter to give a specific answer to the question, the attorney gave up after Walter concluded the discussion with: "Again, I just feel embarrassed to say that I don't know the nature of that task. I have no basis for making a judgment on that."

On the other hand, when Walter was sure about something, he was quite forthright in his claim to knowledge. When the attorney suggested that Walter's report of Tex's slurring of speech when asked to repeat a semi-nonsense phrase was not, in fact, slurring but simply a part of Watson's Texas drawl, Walter acerbically replied: "Though I have not climbed telephone poles, I have talked to many people from Texas and I believe that I'm quite familiar with a Texas drawl. What I heard was above and beyond a Texas drawl. I heard slurring of s's. Difficulty in pronouncing s's."

Even on the topic of drugs and brain damage, Walter provided insight. He stated that part of his job was to determine the cause of brain damage when it occurs and that, primarily by a process of elimination, he believed drugs to be the source of Watson's brain wave abnormalities. He began by stating that drug use was probably the cause but that he could not be sure because he knew neither the amounts, types, or combinations of drugs. Further, there is conflicting evidence about LSD's ability to cause chronic brain damage, though there is clearer, less conflicting information about amphetamines. Walter's final conclusion was: "Our information in 1971 . . . is not so solid that I could make an unequivocal absolute statement that Mr. Watson has a chronic brain syndrome as a result of drugs. In my judgment—it is my best judgment—it is a possibility."

For many attorneys, anxious not so much to determine the truth but to convict or free the defendant, such a reply would be highly unsatisfying. It didn't say enough and it wasn't certain. But when the area of expertise is human behavior and the human mind, the criminal justice system and society would be far better served by experts who have enough humility to know how little they know and how tenuously they know it.

If the experts could not agree about brain damage,

schizophrenia, psychosis, and so on, it is hard to see what they had to offer a jury, and especially a jury in a case whose "heart" was the psychiatric testimony. Everyone knew Tex Watson had been deeply involved in killing those seven people. An extraordinary amount of time and money (though remarkably little common sense) went into his trial. No one there knew nor had any way of knowing what his state of mind had been on the night of the murders. We simply don't know enough to uncover that kind of knowledge. Perhaps we never will know because it may not be scientific information that is needed.

Every psychiatrist who interviewed Watson found him to be a weak, dependent, and passive personality. It is possible that that is the only unanimous point of agreement among these experts. The question that engaged them after that is how much responsibility should weak, dependent, and passive people be required to take when they happened to become embroiled in powerful, independent, and active events such as took place in the turbulent and rebellious sixties,—e.g., LSD and Charles Manson? But that is not a question that research or the empirical method of science can ever answer. It is a deeply moral question that is intricately related to our idea of humanity and our beliefs about the meaning of life. Juries may be a poor vehicle for answering such questions, but they have at least one virtue: they answer the question with full awareness of all their own inherent and human limitations. They must, each and every one, give their opinion and abide by the consequences.

The psychiatric circus at Tex Watson's trial typifies what goes on during the murder trials of defendants who have become famous—or infamous—because of their crimes. Cases that generate massive publicity also include large numbers of psychiatrists. This is, in part, because the factors in the cases that create the publicity also capture the attention of the psychiatrists. But there are other factors as well. Obviously the publicity attendant upon a psychiatrist's appearance at a highly publicized, media-covered trial can be useful to his or her career. The psychiatrist has the opportunity to be a major factor in either an acquittal or a guilty verdict (depending upon his ideological orientation). Famous trials attract a lot of would-be heroes: psychiatrists and lawyers alike.

Without psychiatrists, the Watson trial wouldn't have amounted to much. Tex was a little weak on his recall of events; the women involved all had every reason to be self-serving in their evidence; and the physical evidence of Watson's hand at the center of the murders was abundant. What else could the defense attorney argue about other than Watson's mental state?

When the psychiatrists for both sides, prompted by the lawyers, got hold of that question, double-talk was produced. The tangles and turns of the testimony amply show how little psychiatric knowledge has to offer when it comes to legal questions about mental states and how much it has to offer when it comes to opinions. The psychiatrists in this case couldn't agree on much of anything. The cross-currents and conflicts in their expertise demonstrated that they could not agree on a diagnosis and even those who did agree on one couldn't decide how serious the condition was—for example, whether or not it constituted actual psychosis. They couldn't agree about whether cxcessive drug use caused brain damage or even about what evidence there was on the question. They could not agree on whether Watson had brain damage or even how smart or mentally alert he was.

Psychiatric theory and the "science" of human behavior are, of course, in a very early stage of development, and it is not the fault of psychiatrists that they do not know more or do not have better theories. It is not to their discredit that they cannot predict, diagnose, or treat more reliably, more accurately, and more effectively. They are stuck with the problem of not knowing very much. But it is misleading to bring this clouded information into the courtroom and act as if it were just like any other scientific knowledge, as if it had the validity and internal consistency of mathematics.

Dr. Walter was the only expert witness at this trial who conveyed any sense of the limits of psychiatric, scientific knowledge. His testimony, because of that, is both believable and irrelevant—believable because it defines exactly what its claims are and irrelevant because its claims are so narrow. Dr. Walter, in testifying about the brain damage question, would only speak to the EEG he interpreted at the time he interpreted it. It was evidence only about the time it was given. It said nothing about earlier or later. And it had an error probability. He did not claim abilities to predict or post-dict. He was unwilling to speculate about whether or not Tex could have climbed the telephone pole and cut the wires, but not because he had no opinion. Everyone has or could have an opinion on such a question. It's simply ordinary speculation: Do you think he could do that? What Walter was refusing to give in that instance was an *expert* opinion. He seemed to understand that his opinion as an *expert* was different from his opinion as a *person*. Where he had no genuine expertise, he offered no opinion. Where he had genuine expertise, however, his information was very limited and not very useful.

Tex Watson, the jury, and the public would all have been better served if the experts had declined to testify. If they had something to offer, it was not about Tex Watson's mind in the past. It would have been interesting to know whether they thought he could receive psychiatric treatment and be helped by it. It would have been interesting to hear whether these psychiatrists would have been willing to provide such treatment. These questions are not asked in insanity trials because that is thought not to be relevant to the purpose of the trial. But is that not the central question when there is no real disagreement about whether the defendant committed the act? Did we not create the insanity defense in order to provide different dispositions for the legally sane and the legally insane?

No one ever thought that an insanity acquittal would result in the exoneration and release of the defendant. That happens nowadays, although it didn't happen with Tex Watson. But it wasn't psychiatry that rescued the world from Tex Watson. The jury could tell he was dangerous. It was perhaps chance that he had come under the power of someone like Charles Manson; he might just as easily have become a blindly devoted follower of a charismatic saint. (He has, in prison, become a born-again Christian.) But the jury didn't need psychiatrists to tell them about Watson's weakness. They weren't going to take any chances with him and his uncritical acceptance of leadership. He was dangerous and they gave him the death sentence.* Was he crazy? Did it really matter to the jury? To society? No jury would have sent him anywhere but death row. They didn't want to ever see him on the streets again.

* The subsequent U.S. Supreme Court action that overturned all death sentences left Tex Watson with a life sentence. As a result, he is regularly reviewed for parole. So perhaps the public will see him on the streets one day.

ROBERT TORSNEY

"Happy Working Felony Thanksgiving"

INSANITY DEFENSES ARE MOST PLAUSIBLE IN THOSE CASES where a person who has not previously been involved in legal difficulties finds himself emotionally overwhelmed (or so he and his friends subsequently allege) and in the unexpected or unusual possession of some kind of weapon. Through both his trials and his psychiatric interviews, Leonard Smith denied that he had a gun in the car with him and even that he had ever owned a gun such as the one described by the witnesses to the murder. Dan White claimed he picked up his old police revolver in a kind of trance that began when he heard the unbelievable news that George Moscone was going to double-cross him both casually and publicly. Tex Watson was high on some amazing combination of drugs when, he said, the women who accompanied him placed the weapons in his hands. Even Prosenjit Poddar, who had acquired a gun weeks earlier, hinting that it was purchased to eliminate the problem of Tanya Tarasoff in his life, appeared in his jealous rage at Tanya's doorstep with a kitchen knife, which he did not customarily carry about.

The case of Robert Torsney is perplexingly different from these. Torsney's victim was a young man he had never seen before, did not know, and had no reason to know. Torsney was carrying a gun, as he always did, because he was a New York City policeman. The killing occurred during his work hours when he was sober, alert, and paying attention to details. Torsney had stable employment, was happily married and in good health. But one night he fired his gun at fifteen-year-old Randy Evans from a distance of about twenty inches; the bullet penetrated Randy Evans's brain and killed him almost instantly. After firing the shot, Torsney turned and walked to his car, without making any comment to his two fellow officers about the boy, who lay dying, sprawled across a chain-link fence. A jury found Torsney not guilty by reason of insanity.

On Thanksgiving Day, 1976, Officer Torsney had to work, and he was unhappy about it. At thirty-four, he'd been on the force for eight years and was tired of the conditions. He'd just as soon be at home with his wife and kids on Thanksgiving—just like a regular person. He made a note of his dissatisfaction, for the record, as it were (for the *real* record, as it turned out). At the top of his log book, at the beginning of his work day, he inscribed "Happy Working Felony Thanksgiving." And then he went to work.

In the evening, police headquarters received a call reporting a man with a gun lurking around the residence of the caller. It was the kind of report that could be either trouble or nothing, but there was no way to know which. Officers Robert Faity, Matthew Williams, and Torsney got into their radio car and headed out to Cyprus Houses, a public housing development in the East New York section of Brooklyn. It was getting dark when they arrived at the development to check out the lurking gunman. The officers were appropriately cautious and alert as they made their way to the home of the person who had called in the report. The interview was inconclusive and, after taking down such information as seemed relevant, the police left the building. Officer Torsney unsnapped the leather guard on his pistol holster so that he had ready access to the weapon in case the reported man-with-a-gun was still around and thinking about looking for trouble.

As they came out of the building, several black teenagers were coming up the street toward them. One of them, fifteen-year-old Randy Evans, called out to the policemen, asking if his apartment had been searched. Torsney pulled his gun out of his holster and without taking the time even to extend his arm fully or to call out any kind of warning, he fired at the boy. He was about two feet away from Randy when he fired the gun, and even though he had not had time to aim the weapon properly, the shot fired true. Randy Evans fell backward across a chain-link fence that ran along the sidewalk. Robert Torsney turned and walked back down Fountain Avenue to the radio car parked in the street. He ejected the spent casing and reloaded the gun. (That's something they teach policemen—to reload immediately after firing their weapon. Dan White and Robert Torsney both had learned that lesson well.)

Officer Faity was stunned as he watched the sudden, unexpected shooting. As far as he knew, nothing had precipitated the firing of the gun, and he was standing right there. As Torsney walked away, Officer Faity took charge, called for an ambulance, requested that a police superior be called immediately and informed of the events, and ordered Officer Williams to take Torsney back to the station house—and to do it right away.

In the car, riding to the station, Williams asked Torsney, "What did you do?" Torsney replied, "I don't know, Matty, what did I do?"

If Torsney didn't know at that minute what had happened, he later recalled enough to construct a version that made perfect sense to him. Throughout the trial, which began almost a year later, Torsney insisted that he had acted in self-defense, that he had seen the victim reach into his left side pocket and pull out something silvery that looked like a gun. His own attorney apparently was not impressed by this story, because no gun was found at the scene. (Some bicycle tools were found in the vicinity of the killing, but they were never connected to Randy Evans.) The attorney did not argue self-defense. Instead, he argued that Torsney had an insanity defense because the shooting was a product of a very rare, epileptoid-like brain seizure. The seizure activity was rare all right: not only in the population but also in Torsney's life. Torsney had no medical history of any kind of epilepsy-like problems and had no previous seizures that he or anyone else knew about. It was also so rare that a number of psychiatrists claimed they'd never heard of it. But those claims weren't heard until later.

Yet it was apparently more plausible than Torsney's version of self-defense or the prosecution's version of reckless hostility and fear and second-degree murder. The all-white jury brought in a verdict of not guilty by reason of insanity. In New York, that means that "at the time of such conduct, as a result of mental disease or defect, [a person] lacks substantial capacity to know or appreciate either the nature and consequence of such conduct or that such conduct was wrong." They came to that questionable conclusion after only five hours of deliberation.

Long before the case came to trial, it created a fair amount of citizen unrest. Immediately following the shooting —or as soon as rumor of it had spread through the area— there were "civil disturbances" that were "put down." When the Patrolmen's Benevolent Association assisted Officer Torsney in gaining release from prison pending trial, the Black Police Officers' Association protested the nature of that involvement, charging that it had racist overtones. Randy Evans's parents sued the city of New York for five million dollars, and the New York City Council Ethics Commission had to think about whether there was a conflict of interest if a city councilman, Edward Rappaport, took on the task of defending Officer Torsney on the second-degree murder charge. They decided that there would be no ethical problem. A high-level defense would, presumably, be particularly welcome to the City Council if it got New York out from under the Evans's suit.

In early November 1977 the trial began. It was not a particularly long one as murder trials go, lasting only thirteen days. Many of the witnesses testified only to what they observed at the time of the killing itself, and the testimony of those witnesses was generally consistent with the first newspaper reports of the shooting. They all thought it had been unprovoked. No one but Torsney reported seeing Randy Evans reach in his pocket or have anything silvery in his hands. Bystanders and police officers alike had seen nothing but the boy approaching and Officer Torsney shooting.

Randy's family and friends attended the trial faithfully, anxious to see that justice be done, but fearful that it would not be. Even after a year, they still mourned the loss of their son with the intensity experienced only by those who know that the loss was totally unnecessary.

The prosecution contended that Torsney had shot Randy Evans without provocation when he panicked in a potentially dangerous situation. The fact that he had never previously used his service revolver was introduced. Dr. Herbert Spiegel, Clinical Professor of Psychiatry at Columbia University School of Medicine, testified for the prosecution. Dr. Spiegel had hypnotized Officer Torsney and found that even under hypnosis he repeated his story of seeing Randy Evans pull something silverish from out of his pocket just prior to Torsney's firing his gun. However, Dr. Spiegel concluded that Robert Torsney's mental state did not fit the definition required in New York for an insanity defense. Instead, he thought that Torsney suffered from a "garden variety" neurotic character disorder, with tendencies toward hysterical dissociation (which is to say he forgot or repressed things under stress). Spiegel characterized the gun that Torsney saw as a "mistaken perception," not as a genuine delusion, thus ruling out a diagnosis of psychosis (although there was precious little evidence to suggest any mental defense, let alone psychosis). In conclusion, he assessed the killing simply as the final result of Torsney's panic when he thought he was in danger. In panic, he didn't reflect upon, reason through, or judge his actions. He simply fired his weapon and killed the source of what he saw as a potential threat.

Torsney's sister and wife both testified on his behalf. His sister, Carol Ann, told of the frequent beatings by his father that Robert had endured as a child. The father had been severe with all the children, but particularly violent with Robert. In addition, her brother had been in a motorcycle accident in 1975 that had left him very edgy. She was unable to remember any specific events that showed this edginess, but she was certain that there were differences in her brother's personality after the accident. Torsney's wife also testified about the motorcycle accident and how his behavior had suddenly changed so significantly that they were, for a time, driven to the brink of separation. But there were no medical findings introduced to substantiate this implied claim of physical damage to the brain.

After Torsney's sister and wife testified, City Councilman Rappaport called two expert mental health witnesses: Dr. Joy Roy, a licensed psychologist, and Dr. Daniel Schwartz, Chief of Forensic Psychiatry at King's County Medical Center and one of New York's most frequent psychiatric expert witnesses.

Dr. Roy gave Officer Torsney an IQ test on which he scored only 88, a lower score than one might expect of a police officer. However, another psychologist retested him and Torsney managed a very respectable score of 106, solidly in the average range. After applying her tests, Dr. Roy concluded that Officer Torsney was overcontrolled, prone to sudden outbursts, and afraid of responding to his feelings. She believed that his blanking out right after the shooting and his failure to react appropriately to what he had done were further evidence of how dissociated he was from his feelings. Dr. Spiegel had also made this judgment, but he had stated that such behavior was neurotic; in essence, immature and inappropriate. Dr. Roy suggested that there might be some organic disturbance that would account for these deficits in Robert Torsney's personality. Of course, there could be brain injuries that would account for otherwise quite inexplicable behavior. But one must do more than imagine the possibility. A good defense lawyer must demonstrate genuine physical evidence of physiological defect, and for this purpose, Attorney Edward Rappaport called Dr. Daniel Schwartz to the stand.

Dr. Schwartz is not an unfamiliar figure in New York courtrooms, and it was not unlikely that Rappaport would be anxious to have Schwartz examine his client. Schwartz had been appointed previously by the court to assess the mental state of David Berkowitz, the Son of Sam killer; later, he evaluated Mark David Chapman, who shot and killed John Lennon. In the *Chapman* case, Schwartz would have testified for the defense, but Chapman had a vision commanding him to plead guilty and, as a result, Schwartz testified only in the sentencing phase of the trial.

Schwartz has testified over the past fifteen years in about 350 trials, sometimes for the prosecution, sometimes for the defense. Many critics of forensic psychiatrists say that this willingness to testify for both sides is evidence that they are simply hired guns. Psychiatrists, on the other hand, contend that their willingness to testify on both sides demonstrates their objectivity and impartiality. Schwartz himself contends that "an insanity plea does not depend on psychiatric testimony as much as it does on the likeability of the defendant and on whether the jury thinks he is a danger to the community."

In the case of Robert Torsney, Daniel Schwartz was a most helpful witness. He was helpful in conveying to the jury that the policeman was not a particularly dangerous person to the community—at least to the community that the all-white jury represented. The black community may have thought differently. Schwartz examined Torsney three times. During one of those sessions, Torsney was given an injection of sodium amytol, commonly called truth serum. Under the influence of the drug, Torsney presented the same story that he did in his ordinary state. He recounted seeing the young man reach into his left front pocket and pull out something silvery that looked like a gun. Schwartz concluded that Torsney was engaging in what he called "retrospective falsification," a technical term to explain why Torsney's memory of events was different from that of every other witness. Schwartz's assessment of this "falsification" (which the lay person might well call lying or remembering wrong—both of which are common and neither of which require assessments or fancy explanations) was that the officer had developed a delusion about the event.

Dr. Spiegel, who testified for the prosecution, said Torsney had a mistaken or erroneous perception: he thought he saw a gun, but he was wrong. Dr. Schwartz, for the defense, characterized the same set of events as delusional, a much more serious-sounding description. Torsney did not think he saw a gun and fired at the threatening sight; he fired and afterward invented the gun he supposedly saw in order to explain the firing of his own gun. Furthermore, he persists in believing this memory to be true. It could not, of course, *be* true since there was no gun. Hence, the man has a delusion.

The actual explanation of the firing of the gun (as opposed to the explanation that Torsney had invented) was that Torsney, at the exact moment he thought he saw the silvery gun, suffered a "psychomotor seizure," presumably something like an epilepsy seizure. This seizure, Dr. Schwartz explained, caused Torsney to fire the gun at that unfortunate moment. An EEG was taken of Torsney's brain waves and, unfortunately for the defense, the report of the test interpreted the EEG tracings as being well within the normal range. Dr.

Schwartz did not find that information either a setback or a surprise. He pointed out that there was great variance in EEGs and, in any case, the abnormality would probably show up in the tracing only during an actual attack. The only "evidence" of such an attack during Torsney's entire life was that proffered by Dr. Schwartz when he asserted that an epileptoid-like psychomotor seizure was the only thing that could account for the shooting.

The only thing? The prosecution thought otherwise, of course. Their account was a much simpler one. Torsney, by his own admission, didn't much like blacks. He felt himself to be in danger when he was in the black community, particularly as a white policeman. He was angry that he had to work on Thanksgiving. Angry and scared and with a gun loose in its holster, Torsney was a walking time bomb. When he saw Randy Evans coming toward him, he mistakenly interpreted a movement or gesture by Evans, panicked, and used his gun. In those terms, it was easy enough to understand how the trigger got pulled: nothing more elaborate seemed called for.

But Dr. Schwartz saw it differently. In an interview with a *New York Times* reporter after the trial, he explained that it had taken him almost a year to come to the decision that Torsney's mental status corresponded to the New York law's definition of a condition in which criminal responsibility could not be found. He genuinely believed that Torsney suffered from a rare form of epilepsy called Automatism of Penfield, and therefore was not guilty of homicide.

Torsney agreed with the doctor; at least partially. Like Schwartz he didn't believe he was guilty of homicide for, as he said to Schwartz, "I don't feel guilty like I did anything wrong. I can't say I like black people, but I don't let that affect me. There is a lot of violence down there. My life is in danger." But he did not agree with Dr. Schwartz that he was insane: he believed he acted in self-defense.

In some respects it was the ideal (instead of the customary impossible) Catch-22 situation for the defense. The prosecution kept hammering away that there was no gun and since there was no gun, Torsney could not have acted in self-defense. The defense was in the enviable position of agreeing with the prosecution: *there was no gun.* And as Rappaport stressed in his summation to jury, "If there was no gun, then this man is sick."

Torsney was a decent man, Rappaport contended, and, after he shot Evans and when he did not understand that he had done it because of a seizure, he had invented the gun in Evans's hand. "In order for [Torsney] to be able to go on and survive and live with himself, he placed a gun that wasn't there in the hands of the boy, because to act otherwise would have been an act of insanity." The message was that only a crazy man would shoot an unarmed, fifteen-year-old boy without provocation.

It was as simple as that. If there was a gun, Torsney was not guilty because he had acted in self-defense; if there was no gun, then Torsney was not guilty by reason of insanity because only an insane man would see a gun where there was no gun; only an insane man would have a delusion.

What could the jury do? Torsney seemed such a decent sort. After five hours of deliberation, they found Robert Torsney not guilty by reason of insanity. And then the really perplexing issues in this case began to unfold.

The customary procedure in cases in which a defendant is found not guilty by reason of insanity is to send him to a state mental institution for diagnosis and evaluation of his present mental condition. The jury verdict, of course, refers to his mental status at the time the crime was committed. Generally, it is assumed that the mental condition that resulted in the dangerous behavior is, if not constantly present, at least potentially present so that the "exonerated" defendant is expected to spend some considerable time in a mental facility of some kind until a set of doctors declare him cured. Because he has demonstrated that he is dangerous because of a mental illness, he may be held until treatment renders him no longer dangerous.

In accordance with this view of the verdict, Torsney was sent to the Mid-Hudson Psychiatric Center at the conclusion of his trial. Three months later he was sent to Creedmoor Hospital for diagnosis and evaluation. His attorney announced he would file for a police disability pension on the grounds of mental illness. It sounded rather like the young man who murdered his parents, then threw himself on the mercy of the court because he was an orphan. The black community was outraged. Editorials were written. The state department of mental hygiene continued to evaluate Officer Torsney.

One year to the day after the beginning of Torsney's trial, the news was released that the department of mental hygiene had recommended to the state supreme court in Brooklyn that Torsney be released. They left to the discretion of the court whether the release should be unconditional or whether Torsney should be required to continue outpatient clinic care. They did recommend that he not be permitted to return to police work if it involved walking a beat, but otherwise, they felt the police department could have him back. The court agreed to hold hearings on the department's recommendation.

The formal procedures that result in such a recommendation are considerably complex. First, three psychiatrists on the staff of the facility where the patient is being held must examine him and must all decide that he is not dangerous either to himself or others and therefore should be released. Then the director of the hospital must interview the patient and concur in the recommendation for release. The recommendation must be reviewed by the forensic service group of the hospital and by the state commissioner of mental hygiene. A panel of three psychiatrists from outside the state system of hospitals and clinics is then appointed and they interview the patient and staff at the facility where the patient is housed. Their recommendation is then sent to the court, which has total discretion with respect to acting on the recommendation. Hence, far more care is taken to decide that a person is not dangerous because of mental illness than is often used to determine that a mental illness exists. It is somewhat difficult to imagine how several groups of psychiatrists could uniformly agree about how dangerous Torsney was or was not when the two psychiatrists who appeared at his trial could not agree on whether he was mentally ill. There are many research studies that show that psychiatrists are not very skilled at predicting dangerousness, so variance is likely, but psychiatrists ought to be reliable at diagnosing mental illness if we are to take any of their opinions seriously.

Although it may seem surprising that the psychiatrists reached such agreement about the absence of dangerousness in Robert Torsney, the finding may be more easily understood when the psychiatric reports that accompanied the recommendation are considered. Dr. Deborah Kaiser, chief of the Creedmoor forensic unit, reported that they had found no evidence of psychomotor epilepsy during his time at Creedmoor. "That was never our diagnosis," she pointed out. Further, the Creedmoor doctors contended, during Torsney's stay at the hospital, they had seen no sign of psychosis or brain damage of any kind and no hints of hysterical disassociative reaction. In fact, they found that Torsney suffered from no mental disease since he had been with them. Although they did not say so at that time, the obvious question was, how can they treat a patient for an illness that they don't believe he has and have no reason to believe he has? Although their conclusion was that he was not dangerous, the real import of their assessment was that he wasn't mentally ill.

This perplexing news took the criminal justice system by surprise. Prosecutors and judges were accustomed to the psychiatrists releasing defendants after eight or ten or twenty months when they had provided sufficient treatment for the patient to be able to get along without harming others, which has happened in about one quarter of the not guilty by reason of insanity murder defendants in New York. But the court was not at all sure what to make of the claim that the psychiatrists found no evidence of any mental illness and thus could provide no treatment.

Having already been so well served by experts, the court's first action was to appoint two more psychiatrists to review the state's report. Meanwhile, Torsney's lawyer Rappaport was jockeying for a hearing on the officer's $15,000 a year disability pension before the police department's internal hearing on whether Torsney was fit to be a police officer. The timing was critical because if Torsney was thrown off the force for unfitness (despite the department of mental hygiene's opinion) before the pension hearing, he would probably no longer be eligible for the three-quarter-salary disability pension (for mental illness and "combat fatigue," said his lawyer) that he was seeking.

Judge Leonard Yoswein's court-appointed psychiatrists appeared before him in December 1978, along with sixteen other witnesses, to consider whether Torsney should be released in accordance with the recommendation of the department of mental hygiene. The hearing stretched out over nine days, and witness after witness recounted the same opinion: Torsney was not dangerous now or likely to be a danger to society; that there was no evidence of psychosis, epilepsy, Automatism of Penfield, or hysterical dissociation. There was only evidence of a two-second murder by a man with an "impulsive and explosive" personality. To be impulsive and explosive is surely neither a crime nor a mental illness; it's simply a way of describing people who are short-tempered. In the eighteenth century it was described as a choleric personality and was thought to be one of the four possible personality types. Although theories of personality have changed radically since then, they have not changed so much that short-tempered or impulsive qualities are considered mental illness.

Such a judgment, however, doesn't take into account the thoroughness of psychiatry in tracking down mental illness. The "isolated explosive disorder" has been categorized as a mental disorder, and it is characterized as a "single, discrete episode of failure to resist an impulse that led to a single, violent, externally directed act, which had a catastrophic impact on others." An "intermittent explosive disorder" has also been defined, which differs from the isolated explosive disorder only if it happens more than once. In this case, perhaps the psychiatrists thought that Torsney was the "isolated explosive" type, and thus had already used up his one event.

Whatever the reason, this time they did not believe that his "impulsive and explosive personality" constituted either a threat or a mental illness. One of the newly appointed psychiatrists urged that Torsney be released, receive regular outpatient care after his release, and not be allowed to carry a gun. Such a recommendation made some sense to the judge, but we are left with a lingering question about the purpose of the outpatient treatment. If the psychiatrists could find no evidence of mental illness, what was he to be treated for? Did those who urged continuing treatment think Torsney should be taught not to be impulsive? Or that regular psychotherapy is probably good for everyone and in any case it wouldn't hurt? Or did they believe that there had been a remarkable error in Torsney's trial? Did they think that there had been a miscarriage of justice and that continuing psychiatric care could be a kind of punishment in lieu of the *real* punishment that Torsney had evaded through the fraudulent insanity defense? Dr. Milton Hollar, the court-appointed psychiatrist, urged continuing psychiatric treatment "because of the incident." That is, because Torsney had killed someone. It *sounded* like punishment.

Judge Yoswein's verdict in the case was not unexpected, given the testimony he heard. Torsney was released from Creedmoor Hospital. He was not permitted to carry a gun or to be a police officer or any other kind of peace officer. He was to receive continuing outpatient treatment at Creedmoor for five years. Judge Yoswein pointed out that the evidence consistently showed that the sizable number of psychiatrists who had examined Torsney had found no evidence of mental illness, but he did not discuss what, during the forthcoming five years of treatment, the doctors were to treat. He did explain that "we cannot simply throw away the key on patients who have at one time been found not guilty by reason of mental illness or defect and commit them to an institution as a result thereof." Officer Torsney had been at Creedmoor for about nine months. He spent long weekends at home. It is hard to imagine that his experience so far could be characterized as "throwing away the key."

The district attorney immediately appealed Judge Yoswein's ruling to the appellate court, which consisted of a panel of five judges. The appellate court stayed the order for two weeks, which resulted in Torsney's remaining in Creedmoor Hospital. In mid-January they heard arguments on the request for release and were appalled. Prior to handing down a decision, the chief justice himself commented, "I'm not overly impressed with any of the evidence in this case."

When the appellate court made its unanimous ruling in a twenty-page decision, it was sharply critical of the mental health system which, it asserted, had merely "warehoused" Officer Torsney and had never even prepared a treatment plan for him and had never administered individual care. They charged that the state's attempts to find and treat the patient's illness were a "glaring failure." Despite their outrage, we might ask whether the problem was that the psychiatrists failed to find the illness or that the patient failed to have one?

The seeds of the charge that the state had been lax were heard during the hearing before the court when Alfred Annenberg, the representative of the state department of mental hygiene, had pointed out that it was not the state's fault that the jury had found Torsney not guilty by reason of insanity. When the justices suggested that the state had not looked properly into Torsney's rare form of epilepsy, Annenberg replied that "before this trial, I never heard of Automatism of Penfield," and that he "would have had four experts to testify there's no such thing," had he been at the trial.

It was argument at cross-purposes. The outraged justices complained that no treatment was given for Torsney's problem, while the put-upon state argued that there was no illness to treat and, that if Torsney had a problem, it wasn't mental illness. It was as if the judges believed that since the jury found that there was a mental illness, then a mental illness did exist, because juries are the deciders of facts in criminal trials. The doctors hadn't treated Torsney's epilepsy and, in any case, he did have an explosive, impulsive personality. Surely they could do something about that, said the panel of judges somewhat sanctimoniously. "We may not shirk our responsibility to the community by prematurely releasing Mr. Torsney while he continues to suffer from a dangerous personality disorder." The state, said the judges, must give Torsney "an opportunity to surmount his dangerous personality disorder and resume his place in the community." The dangerous personality disorder was, presumably, that Torsney was generally found to be impulsive and short-tempered. Torsney himself admitted that he was impulsive, but the claim that the "personality disorder" was dangerous was another matter. What were the state therapists to do? Torsney was not to be released; he was to be treated for something.

Within twenty-four hours, the state department of mental hygiene announced that it would appeal the decision of the appellate panel to the state supreme court, which in New York is called the Court of Appeals. Edward Rappaport, Torsney's lawyer, also intended to appeal the decision, though his reasoning was not entirely compatible with the contentions of the mental hygiene department.

Rappaport's claim, in essence, was that he and Torsney had played the game fairly and won the acquittal and that the state could not require Torsney to serve time in a hospital as if he'd been found guilty. The mental hygiene people, on the other hand, were arguing that the court created the problem by allowing dubious insanity defenses and that it couldn't and shouldn't expect the mental hygiene department to pick up the pieces for the legal system when the court had created the problem.

"If he's not clinically ill, what are you going to treat?" inquired one state official. The appellate court's decision suggests that if the psychiatrists didn't believe the jury's diagnosis of epilepsy, then perhaps they would prefer to believe the appellate court's diagnosis of a "dangerous personality disorder." The psychiatrists in the mental hygiene department rejected that diagnosis as well, feeling that neither judges nor juries were qualified diagnosticians. A date was set for arguments before the Court of Appeals.

Officer Torsney was to stay at Creedmoor, but, in actuality, he didn't stay there much of the time. The Creedmoor psychiatrists were reluctant to muddle the situation by releasing Torsney in violation of the appellate court's order. Such an action, for which they could be held personally responsible, might also affect the hearing before the state supreme court, where they hoped to be vindicated. The Creedmoor psychiatrists' position was that the law required them to hold a person only if he posed a danger and that to force them to hold a person who was not dangerous was illegal. Therefore, they believed they should be permitted to release the nondangerous Torsney.

On the other hand, they could obey the court's orders by preparing an individual treatment program that would ensure the safe return of Officer Torsney to the community, just as the judges had demanded. The treatment plan they concocted included visits home as part of a rehabilitative program. His rehabilitation, it turned out, was going just fine, and he was spending most nights and weekends at home with his wife and children. Creedmoor coyly referred to this as "reduced custody."

The Court of Appeals, the highest court in the state, heard the arguments in the case promptly. They listened to the state department of mental hygiene, the district attorney, and Torsney's new lawyer, Joseph Frost. Only six justices were sitting at the time and they deadlocked. Reargument was ordered for the following month, when the seventh justice had taken his seat. The arguments were repeated with, according to the *New York Times*, "unusually vociferous questioning" by the justices. The questions of the justices, though to the point, seem amazingly naive. One asked if there had not been a miscarriage of justice, if "the jury might have concluded that he was insane when he was not." And if so, what should the Court do? Another asked if the expert testimony meant that "under stress, [Torsney] could do the same thing again . . . isn't that symptomology?" The latter question shows the problem of psychiatric expertise when it attempts to talk about causative factors in behavior. Everything begins to sound like symptoms of mental disorder simply because it is described as being associated with undesirable behavior.

Officer Torsney continued his visits home and awaited the decision from the six-week trial conducted by the police commission in February and March. He had been suspended from the force earlier, but the trial was to determine whether the suspension would be official and permanent. The decision was made public two weeks after the Court of Appeals heard the second round of arguments, but before their decision was handed down. The police commission found Torsney guilty of conduct unbecoming an officer and ordered him dismissed from the force. Torsney's lawyers immediately announced that they would appeal this decision too, arguing that the police had ignored the jury verdict that the officer was insane when the Evans boy was killed. It probably didn't help Torsney's case much that, during the months the police commission's decision was being made, the department of mental hygiene was regularly announcing that, as far as they could tell, Torsney had never had any mental illness or defect. The dismissal also made him ineligible for his $15,000 a year pension.

A few weeks later, in mid-July, the Court of Appeals handed down its final decision. The decision "in the Matter of Robert Torsney, the State Commissioner of Mental Hygiene and the King's County District Attorney" was a four to three split. The Court of Appeals overturned the appellate decision and ordered the release of former police officer Torsney.

Justice Matthew Jasen, writing the plurality opinion, concluded reluctantly that "on the present record it is clear that appellant suffers from neither a mental illness or defect nor a personality disorder which renders him dangerous to himself or others. He should, therefore, be released." Creedmoor Hospital released the much-argued-about patient immediately, and Robert Torsney went home to stay, two years and seven months after the Thanksgiving night when he shot and killed Randy Evans.

The Court of Appeals was sharply divided in its decision. As a matter of law, courts that review cases after they have been tried do not reconsider the facts of the case. The facts, except in unusual circumstances, such as when critical and new evidence becomes known, are established at the trial court level. Because of this, it was not possible for any of the courts that reviewed the Torsney case to say, in effect, "Wait a minute, there's been a mistake. This guy wasn't insane." They were compelled to accept the decision of not guilty by reason of insanity.

The opinion issued by the Court of Appeals had spent some time discussing whether the verdict meant that Torsney was proved to be insane by mental illness or defect or, more simply, whether the verdict meant that the state had failed to prove that he definitely was sane. If the latter were the case, then Torsney might or might not have been insane at the time he committed the crime. That is, the jury found Torsney not guilty by reason of insanity because they weren't certain beyond a reasonable doubt that he was legally sane when he pulled the trigger, although he might have been.

To the nonlegal mind, a verdict of not guilty by reason of insanity sounds as if a defendant had been found to be *insane* and even some of the justices thought that might be the case. However, the alternative interpretation—that Torsney might or might not have been sane but the jury couldn't be sure which—fit the case better. It was surely less awkward to deal with substantial suggestions—if not evidence—that Torsney had never had any mental illness or defect, if the original jury verdict could be interpreted as simply stating the jury's uncertainty about Torsney's mental state.

If the issue of Torsney's sanity and the apparently contradictory jury verdict could be disposed of in that way, then the justices were left only with the question of whether or not Torsney could be held as an involuntary patient in a mental hospital. That question was relatively easy to resolve, since the statutes in this area of the law are fairly clear and frequently interpreted. In New York, as in many other states, an individual may be held and treated in a mental hospital against his wishes only if, as a result of a mental illness or defect, he is a danger to himself or to others. The critical phrase in these laws is "as a result of mental illness or defect." That is, the dangerousness must be a direct result of a mental illness or defect.

Another critical aspect of the involuntary commitment laws is that treatment must be provided if people are being held in hospitals or other institutions and are thus being deprived of their freedom when they have either caused no harm to others or caused no harm for which they could be held responsible.

In Robert Torsney's case, the plurality justices concluded that there was no evidence that he was now suffering from any identifiable mental illness or disorder and that his mental state *now* was the only issue. Whatever his mental state had been at the time of Randy Evans's death was irrelevant, since the trial court jury had already decided, or at least disposed of, that issue. If Torsney had no mental illness or mental defect now, then he could not be held in the state mental hospital, even if everyone thought he indeed might be dangerous. They reiterated the point several times: his dangerousness must be the result of mental illness or defect.

Justice Jasen recounted at considerable length the testimony and reports of psychiatrists and psychologists who had examined Torsney. Since Dr. Daniel Schwartz was heard on the topic at the trial, not one single expert had been heard to say that Torsney had a mental illness or defect. Some had pointed out a personality disorder, but that was just a way of discussing Torsney's impulsiveness and his short temper, not a declaration of mental illness.

Following the logic of Justice Jasen, there was no possible decision other than to order the release of this patient. A legitimate court had found Torsney not guilty and involuntary commitment in a mental hospital could not be used as a form of extrajudicial punishment.

Justice Sol Wachtler, writing for the three dissenting justices, disagreed entirely. It was his opinion that Torsney's continuing dangerousness mandated that he be held to protect the public safety. In addition, he believed that the dangerousness need not be treatable in order to justify the hospital confinement. Wachtler argued that the vagaries of psychiatry—its changing ideas of what constitutes a mental illness or mental defect and its inconsistencies and contradictions—were not appropriate guidelines for the law. He pointed out that when the experts were asked what would happen in the future if Torsney were faced with the same circumstances, they had been unable to say he would not shoot. Some experts had even suggested (and Wachtler was inclined to agree with them) that Torsney in 1979 was exactly the same person he had been in 1976, neither more nor less crazy.

To Justice Wachtler's thinking, one was not dealing with whether or not a person *might* be dangerous; Robert Torsney had demonstrated that he was dangerous, because, without provocation, he had shot to death an unarmed fifteen-year-old boy. How much more evidence of dangerousness did one need?

Justice Wachtler agreed with the psychiatrists who said that Torsney did not have good "impulse control." He did not, however, care whether lack of impulse control was called a mental illness, a mental defect, a personality disorder, a neurotic adaptation, or a bad habit. He simply did not feel that society should be exposed to Robert Torsney's poor impulse control, particularly since one life had already been lost to it. In the justice's opinion, when Robert Torsney could demonstrate that he had good impulse control, then it would be soon enough to bring him back into the world. How he might ever demonstrate that was, of course, unclear.

High court decisions make good reading when there are divided opinions, for each view seems compelling, even though they reach contradictory conclusions. But each view is usually based on a different set of assumptions and, as a result, they differ in how they characterize and highlight the question and choose its relevant aspects.

In the case of Robert Torsney, the New York Court of Appeals' divergent opinions turn on the question of the defendant's guilt. When Justice Jasen and the other justices in the majority argued for Torsney's release, they took as a fact that he was considered not guilty of any crime. Their interpretation of the jury verdict emphasized the "not guilty"—the "by reason of", for all practical purposes, was not relevant at that time. By contrast, Justice Wachtler and the two concurring justices in the minority viewed the not guilty verdict as a conditional one. Torsney was not guilty only because of his insanity, and as a result, the not guilty is only a technical verdict. Torsney was obviously guilty in the sense that all agreed that he committed the act. It is *that* guilt with which the minority justices were concerned.

Seen in this light, the opposing opinions made sense. Those who believed Torsney was guilty urged that he be held by the state; those who believed he was not guilty ordered the state to release him. Such positions are entirely consistent, but they leave society with the same question that it faced on Thanksgiving of 1976. Was Robert Torsney guilty of murdering Randy Evans or was he guilty only of killing Randy Evans? If he was guilty of the murder, then the criminal justice system might appropriately impose punishment, for such guilt implies knowledge and intent. But if we cannot be certain about knowledge and intent, if we cannot be certain of murder but can only be sure of killing, then what follows? If one has only *killed,* is that nothing for which one must be accountable? Robert Torsney lost about one and a half years of his life to the mental health and criminal justice systems. Randy Evans lost his life.

Robert Torsney may well believe to this day that, as he said at his trial, he doesn't "feel guilty, like [he did] anything wrong." Justice Jasen ordered him to be released because he didn't know whether Torsney was *guilty* of anything; Justice Wachtler knew he was guilty of shooting Evans. It is a different sense of *guilt.*

Most of the psychiatrists in this case—and particularly those in the state department of mental hygiene—used Robert Torsney's plight as a pointed example of the problems and especially the potential inconsistencies inherent in an insanity defense. Through their testimony and other public statements, they urged the courts and legislators to take another look at the situation, one that can only contribute to greater public scorn of both the psychiatric profession and the criminal justice system.

Neither the court nor the legislature responded to the challenge. The *New York Times* counseled that "distress over the case" should not "lead to wholesale revision of New York's insanity laws . . . [for] the basic concept of an insanity defense remains fundamental to a humane, responsible system of justice."

It may be true that the basic concept of the insanity defense is fundamental to justice, but it is equally true that such a fundamental idea can be altered, perverted, and abused in practice. In California the *Dan White* case led the state legislature to reconsider the insanity defense and to eliminate the diminished capacity defense. In New York a legislative proposal was made to introduce a new plea of guilty but insane—but nothing came of it.

Surely many of New York City's residents believed that

Torsney was exonerated because the jury was white, the victim was black, and the defendant was a policeman. That is not an impossible explanation because a disproportionately large number of people who receive insanity acquittals are policemen. Yet it is unlikely that the jurors who voted not guilty would agree to that characterization of their verdict. It is improbable that their motives were consciously racist.

They did, after all, have the testimony of two expert mental health witnesses, one of whom was sure that Torsney had brain damage, and the other willing to assert that Torsney possibly had brain damage. The Automatism of Penfield helped to explain the shooting. And it must have been otherwise difficult for the jury to figure out why the shooting had taken place. Why shoot when there was no threat? Brain damage at least offered some reasonable explanation of events.

We can only assume that Dr. Schwartz and Dr. Roy testified in good faith as to their beliefs. That Dr. Schwartz took almost a year to decide that Torsney should not be considered legally responsible suggests the weakness of the evidence for his belief. The jury may well have believed the doctors' versions simply because they wanted to. They doubtless felt sympathy and compassion for Robert Torsney. Not wanting to send him to prison, they might well have thought a stay in a mental hospital would be a less stigmatizing and more acceptable consequence for him. If we were to decide about the fate of any individual for whom we felt sympathy and we had to choose between prison and hospital, which one of us would not choose the hospital? Like most juries, they would have believed that Torsney would receive care and treatment over a long period of time.

What would have helped in this case would have been some early contribution by the state department of mental hygiene. Had state psychiatrists examined Torsney and testified how little they would offer in the state facilities to which he would be sent, the jurors might have come to a very different conclusion about an acquittal by reason of insanity.

The therapists who provide evaluation and treatment in state facilities are seldom asked their opinion in insanity plea cases. Expert psychiatric witnesses, especially the well-known ones, are much more likely to be academicians, administrators of large hospitals, or directors of forensic clinics and not those who would actually provide treatment for insanity acquittees. If jurors voting for insanity acquittals are choosing hospitalization as an alternate form of punishment, they should at least know whether the prospect of treatment (as punishment) is a reality.

The *Torsney* case also demonstrates another aspect of the foolishness engendered by the insanity defense. In the trial itself the defense attorney argued that Torsney was mentally ill; the prosecutor argued that he was not. Through the post-verdict hearings and appeals, the defense attorney argued that Torsney was not mentally ill; the prosecution was now obliged to argue that he was. Although it is true that the trial argument involved assessments of the defendant's sanity at the time of the killing and the posttrial disputes were about the nature of the defendant's current state of mind, the inconsistency is still important. It suggests that we believe insanity is something that comes and goes quixotically—now you have it, now you don't—and its appearance or disappearance is unrelated to any other event. Surely the historical acceptance of the insanity defense depends upon the defendant's being afflicted with a condition that was more serious and integral to his being than something that struck only once. The idea of the insanity defense demands a substantial definition of mental illness. It demands that mental illness be a grave condition that permeates one's life, and not a will-of-the-wisp momentary lack of impulse control. Such weakness of definition demeans the very idea of personal responsibility.

Because psychiatrists are trained to see mental illness and abnormal behavior, that is how they talk about their observations. The American Association of Psychiatry and Law recently recommended to the American Psychiatric Association that they include in further editions of the *Diagnos-*

tic and Statistical Manual a statement about the difference between psychiatric and legal concepts of mental illness. If juries are to be permitted to hear psychiatrists, they should also be instructed about those differences.

If racial motives lay behind Robert Torsney's insanity acquittal, the jury was at least able to hide behind a belief that the acquittal would result in "hospital punishment." Had they voted an insanity acquittal in the face of testimony by the state department of mental hygiene psychiatrists that Torsney needed no treatment, was not dangerous, and would be immediately released, they still might have voted for the insanity acquittal. But then, there would be no question of their motives. The insanity defense provides a shield for jurors to hide behind in such instances.

The inconsistent and conflicting concepts of the insanity defense also provide easy excuses and exits for defendants like Robert Torsney. He went home after two and a half years of legal involvement. His plan was to go to court in order to appeal his dismisal from the police force, to recover his back pay, and to be granted a $15,000-a-year medical disability pension. He had learned how to use the legal system and, like anyone with a surprise jackpot, he was right back for another try to beat the odds—and to defeat justice.

JAMES GRIGSON

The "Hanging Psychiatrist"

OVER THE PAST ONE HUNDRED YEARS, PSYCHIATRISTS, PSYchoanalysts, psychologists, and others in the mental health field have been thrust further and further into every aspect of our public and even our private lives. If they are not the principle decision makers, they are likely to stand next to the presiding officer, making official recommendations. Because life is hard, society has designated mental health practitioners as the experts on all of life's problems.

You want a divorce? The court or your attorney will refer you to "counselors" who can decide whether yours is a truly hopeless case and where you went wrong. Does someone think you've been acting a little unusual lately? A psychiatrist, in a brief exam, will decide whether you are likely to be dangerous to yourself or someone else or perhaps whether you just need treatment. Do you want to be a policeman? Liberals urge you to have a psychiatric exam. Do you want to run for president? Senate? Congress? Many in the therapeutic community urge that all candidates for public office have psychiatric exams and that the results be made public prior to elections.

It would seem to be an impressive safeguard to have these mind specialists (33,000 psychiatrists in the United States, with Los Angeles and New York City having more than their share) checking out our character, personality, and rationality, and making sure that things stay on an even keel. But it doesn't work.

Both within the field of psychiatry and within the medical profession, there is continuing argument and disappointment about psychiatry's failure to be sufficiently scientific. Occasionally, a well-known, highly respected psychiatrist will acknowledge that the practice of psychiatry not only is but should be more an art than a science. But that is not a popular point of view among members of the profession. The development of new drugs and the hope and belief that mental disorders will be controlled eventually by physiological-chemical intervention have given new hope for the scientific status of psychiatry. But initial discoveries have not led to accurate and predictable treatment models, and drug treatment, in most cases, is trial and error, often with regard both to a specific drug and specific dosage.

But if psychiatrists have had difficulty gaining the respect they feel they deserve from the medical community, as well as from society, they have been eminently successful in gaining access and decision-making power in many social institutions and legal forums. In many public settings, the psychiatrist is viewed as the expert on sanity and responsibility. Psychiatrists, however (and allied mental health professionals), while not reluctant to offer themselves as official societal problem solvers, have begun to backtrack in at least one area.

Lawyers and psychiatrists, more often than not, have been at war with one another, but they have made some temporary alliances in order to try to keep psychiatrists from presenting their opinions in some criminal trials. The American Psychiatric Association has decided it should withdraw some of its aid to the courts. It has done so while admitting and insisting on its inability to know enough about the human mind to offer proper or justifiable expertise. It is a new sound of humility. Some have suggested that this retreat acknowledges a new realization by psychiatrists that they had overstepped the boundaries of their knowledge; others suggest that it is a single-issue retreat bound up with the fact that most psychiatrists oppose capital punishment; still others—more cynical psychiatrists—argue that it is an economic action of self-interest in which psychiatry is prepared to give up its role in one small area in order not to be held legally liable and financially responsible for the same role in a much larger area.

The focus of these concerns is a Texas psychiatrist named James Grigson and the case of *Estelle* v. *Smith*. One night in September 1973 Ernest Benjamin Smith, Jr., and Howie Ray Robinson held up a convenience store in Dallas. Both Smith and Robinson were carrying guns. During the holdup the cashier made a sudden move. Smith saw the move and fired his gun, yelling at the same time, "Look out, Howie" (or something like that). Robinson then fired his gun straight at the cashier. The cashier fell to the floor and the two robbers cleaned out the cash drawer and fled.

A short time later the Dallas police caught up with the two men and charged them both with felony-murder. Such a charge is one designed to discourage any criminal activity that might result in death. In essence, if anyone takes part in a felony, during which or because of which someone dies, that person is guilty of homicide. Thus, if three people attempt a bank robbery with a cap pistol, and a bank patron has a heart attack and dies while the robbery is going on, the robbers are all liable for homicide. Similarly, if someone drives a murderer to his victim, the driver is as guilty of the homicide as the one who did the killing—even if the driver never left the car or saw the victim. The logic of the charge is that if it had not been for the lesser crime, the death would never have occurred and, therefore (1) all the participants are as guilty of the person's death as if they had specifically and personally caused it to happen, and (2) they are equally responsible regardless of who (or what) actively caused the death because they acted as a group or as a unit in committing the lesser crime.

Smith and Robinson were tried separately on felony-murder charges. Because a death sentence is possible on such a charge, the judge in the case ordered Smith to submit to a competency evaluation, even though no one, including Smith's lawyer, suggested that Smith was anything but competent. When the competency hearing became a problem later on, the judge explained that he ordered the hearing simply as a precaution, because he didn't want anyone complaining, especially if Smith were found guilty and sentenced to death, on appeal that the defendant was too crazy to have participated properly in the trial. He was, in his view, simply practicing a little defensive judging.

The order was made over the phone and a court-appointed psychiatrist undertook to perform a competency evaluation on Smith. The doctor appeared at the county jail where Smith was being held and spent about ninety minutes with the alleged murderer. He explained that he was a psychiatrist and had been asked by the judge to evaluate Smith's competency to stand trial. Smith was polite, pleasant, and responsive, and cooperated fully with the psychiatrist. During this time, the doctor conducted a five-part exam: (1) general appearance and behavior, (2) production of thought, (3) affect/mood, (4) content of thought, and (5) orientation to time, place, and person.

The general appearance segment, according to the doctor, was "simply observation of how the person walks into the interview room, the way they sit, the attention or lack of attention to personal appearance." In particular, the doctor used this information to determine whether the person was or seemed depressed, agitated, or anxious. The "production of thought" segment involved having Smith talk, after which the doctor decided whether he made sense, whether his thought was linear, or, conversely, whether it was confused, circular, or obsessive. The affect/mood evaluation attempted to determine whether *how* Smith talked about something matched the subject of his talk. Thus, when talking about a pleasant experience, the person's voice and physical demeanor should reflect the positive quality of the experience. In the "content of thought" segment, Smith was asked about his past and present. The final segment, the "orientation," attempted to determine if Smith knew who he was, where he was, when it was, and whether he could focus, concentrate, and remember from moment to moment what was happening. On the basis of this five-part test, the psychiatrist sent a letter to the judge, indicating that he had conducted the examination and had found Ernest Benjamin Smith, Jr., competent to stand trial.

Smith's attorney was never informed by the court or by the psychiatrist that this competency evaluation had taken place. If he had known, he might have attempted to stop it, or he might have insisted on being present during it. Or he might have taken it at face value and let it happen just as it did. What harm could a competency hearing do to Smith? Any statements he made about the crime itself could not be introduced as evidence in the trial, and if he were found incompetent, he wouldn't have to stand trial. But the attorney knew there was no question of Smith's being found incompetent.

During the trial Smith's attorney was given a list of all the witnesses the prosecution expected to call, as was required by law. He was also given access to prosecution files on the case. It was in these files that he found a copy of the letter stating that Smith was competent to stand trial. He could not have been happy to find that the evaluation had been conducted by Dr. James Grigson, the Dallas psychiatrist the press was fond of referring to as "the hanging psychiatrist" and "the killer shrink." The attorney checked the witness list. Grigson's name was not on it, neither as a witness in the guilt phase of the trial nor in the penalty phase, so the attorney probably thought that the competency hearing could not harm his client.

Under Texas law, a case that might result in the death penalty is tried in two parts, in what is called a bifurcated trial. During the guilt phase of the trial, the jurors decide whether or not the defendant is guilty. If they find him guilty, the penalty phase is then held, in which they decide on the basis of additional evidence whether to order the death penalty or a term of imprisonment. In order to decide for the death penalty, a Texas jury must consider three factors: (1) whether the murder was deliberate; (2) whether the defendant's conduct was unreasonable in response to the provocation; and (3) whether the defendant is likely to repeat his violent deeds in the future. If the jury answers "yes" to all three questions after they have heard the additional evidence, then the death penalty is automatic. If all three are answered *no*, then only a prison sentence can be given.

Smith was found guilty in the first phase of the trial, which was not a great surprise. His attorney's hopes were pinned on the penalty phase. Smith had several things going for him. First, his only previous conviction had been for possession of less than an ounce of marijuana. He had been charged with some other, more serious crimes, but since he was never found guilty, those charges could not be brought before the jury in this trial. Second, Smith had not done the actual shooting. Third, although he had been carrying a gun, the weapon had misfired and there was some evidence that Smith knew the gun was defective. There was conflicting testimony as to whether Smith had said, "Get him, Howie" (the "him" referring to the cashier) or "Look out, Howie." Therefore, there was a reasonable chance that they could get "no's" from the jury on all three questions.

When the penalty phase began, the prosecution offered no witnesses but requested permission to reopen, which meant that the prosecution could later request the introduction of further testimony. The court granted permission. Smith's attorney called three witnesses, each of whom testified to Smith's good character. The testimony was brief and to the point. Once the defense rested, the prosecution wanted to exercise its request to reopen. They had only one witness. The judge agreed. Smith's attorney could hardly believe it when he heard that the one witness they wished to call was Dr. James Grigson.

He objected. He objected strenuously and lengthily. First of all, he had never requested a mental examination of Smith; second, the examination had been conducted without his being informed; third, the results of the exam had not been made available to him; fourth, the purpose of the exam was a competency evaluation, not a penalty recommendation; fifth, Smith had not been told that his statements to Grigson could be used against him at the trial; sixth, Smith had been denied counsel during this evaluation; and seventh, the prosecuting attorney had concealed his plan to have Grigson testify at the trial by omitting his name from the witness lists.

The judge listened to his long list of objections and overruled them all with the warning that Grigson was not to testify to any of the specific statements that Smith had made, and that he could only testify to his opinion on the matter at hand, an opinion that Grigson had come to as a result of listening to Smith's statements. The primary focus of Grigson's testimony to the jury was whether the defendant was likely to repeat his violent deeds in the future. This was not an easy question, since there was no record of previous violent deeds, but Dr. Grigson had little problem with the query. He stated that Smith would repeat his violent deed again and again and again, that violence was all Ernest Benjamin Smith, Jr., knew, and that Smith was now, and always would be, a psychopath, a sociopath, and a man without a conscience. The jury came back with a death sentence.

James Grigson, M.D., has a private psychiatric practice in Dallas. He is a local boy and a graduate of Baylor and Southwestern Medical School (now part of the University of

Texas Health Science Center at Dallas) who did his psychiatric residency at Parkland and Timberlawn hospitals in Dallas. Although he has been accused by a University of Texas law professor of "operating at the brink of quackery," his credentials are in order. He is certified by the American Board of Neurology and Psychiatry and was for some years on the medical faculty of Southwestern Medical School. He has been conducting examinations of criminals since the mid-sixties and, after fifteen years, he estimates that he has interviewed over 8,000 men and women charged with crimes. He has participated in numerous trials and is respected by defense lawyers who have reason to know him to be a formidable witness.

Physicians, including psychiatrists, are often uncomfortable in the courtroom. One physician has suggested this is because the doctor is not in control of the situation. This may be at least part of the explanation. The psychiatrist frequently bristles or becomes defensive under the harsh cross-examination that the adversary method of the courtroom requires. Often, he sounds as if he believes he is being picked on unduly by the attorneys, and he begins to react emotionally, frequently claiming far more certainty than his knowledge genuinely allows. If the opposing attorney is able to provoke him sufficiently, the psychiatrist sooner or later will leap out on the proverbial limb and the lawyer will obligingly cut him down.

An additional cause of psychiatrists' discomfort in the courtroom may be that juries are generally thought to be hostile to them. The psychiatrist often speaks a technical language or a jargon that the juror does not understand. He often appears to be patronizing the jurors, and may be from a different social class than that of the jurors. One criminal defense attorney pointed out that psychiatrists will come into court in weird clothing—for example, a suit, no tie, and tennis shoes—setting themselves apart from and frequently alienating the jury. But none of that is typical of James Grigson.

At forty-eight, Grigson is a tall, soft-spoken witness. He always dresses appropriately, like a business or professional man. He is affable, at ease, and confident about his opinions. He explains the examination he gives to the defendant in simple ordinary language, which is appropriate because it's a simple ordinary examination. He states his conclusions with a minimum of psychiatric jargon. He is a model of humility and sincerity. The jury responds very positively to him, since he is not a hired gun, available at a price to mouth any opinion. Jim Grigson really believes what he testifies to, and what he testifies to in more and more cases is that the defendant should receive the death penalty because he is, in Grigson's own language, a sociopath, a man without conscience who will go on throughout his life performing violent acts in his own self-interest. The defendant, Grigson frequently says, is as bad a sociopath as one can be and therefore can't get any worse; but he won't get better either, for psychiatry has nothing to offer the sociopath.

Jim Grigson has testified to the sociopathic personality of the defendant in about sixty capital murder cases in Texas. With one or two exceptions, the jury sentenced the defendant to death, primarily and often exclusively on the basis of Grigson's testimony.

In 1974, when Ernest Benjamin Smith, Jr.'s, attorney objected to Dr. Grigson's testifying during the penalty phase, Grigson had not yet acquired the reputation he has today. But it was well known even then that having Jim Grigson against you was bad news. Grigson says that he doesn't testify *for* anyone. He just tells what he believes to be the truth. He has been hired by federal judges; attorney generals; U.S. attorneys; judicial district judges from Texas, Arizona, and Alaska; district attorneys; and defense attorneys. The defense attorneys who hate to see him on the other side would love to have him on their team because he is such a formidable, unflappable witness. Having Grigson for your witness is like having the only wild card in a poker game; he makes you look like a sure winner.

Grigson's reputation with the press is as a prosecution witness, but he himself points out that in about one-third of the death penalty examinations he conducts, his judgment is not useful to the prosecution because he believes there is hope for the defendant. Newspaper accounts stress that he always testifies to the unredeemable nature and character of the defendant, but of course if he were not prepared to testify to that, the prosecution would not call him to the stand.

His testimony in all these cases is remarkably similar. He describes the five-part, all-purpose examination he conducts and then states his opinion that, based on that exam, the defendant is a sociopath. He then describes and defines sociopathy and explains that it is (a) incurable and (b) not a mental illness of any sort. He postulates a scale of one to ten and places the victim at ten. He speaks with certainty. When asked by the defense lawyer if he is ever wrong about such judgments, he acknowledges that he is sometimes wrong, "but," he continues, "in this case I'm not."

He was absolutely certain about his judgment of Ernest Benjamin Smith, Jr. After explaining that Smith was a severe sociopath (up there at ten on the scale), the prosecuting attorney asked whether Grigson thought Smith felt any guilt or remorse, whether, in effect, Smith had any conscience.

A. No. He has none.
Q. Now. Dr. Grigson, what is your prognosis in this case?
A. Oh, he will continue his previous behavior—that which he has done in the past. He will do it in the future.
Q. All right. So, were he released into society, I take it, then, you would not expect his behavior to differ from what it has been?
A. No. If anything, it would only get worse.
Q. Now, Dr. Grigson, this sociopathic personality that Smith has—is this a condition that will improve with time? I guess what I'm asking you is this: Is this a stage that he is passing through that he will grow out of?
A. No. This is not what you would consider a stage. This

is a way of life. Just as you work every day, well, his personality comes out in his behavior, but it is not a stage he is going through. It's only something he will continue.

Q. You said get worse?

A. Yes.

Q. If it can?

A. Right . . . It's my opinion that really, Mr. Smith does not have any regard for another human being's property or for their life, regardless of who it may be. This is what makes him such a very severe sociopath. He has complete disregard for another human being's life.

Q. Dr. Grigson, does the field of medicine—perhaps psychiatric treatment and/or hospitalization of some sort—does that have anything beneficial to offer someone like Ernest Benjamin Smith?

A. We don't have anything in medicine or psychiatry that in any way at all modifies or changes this behavior. We don't have it. There is no treatment, no medicine, nothing that's going to change this behavior.

Q. Now, Dr. Grigson, do you have an opinion as to whether or not there is a possibility that the defendant, Ernest Benjamin Smith, will commit criminal acts of violence that will constitute a continuing threat to society?

A. Yes sir, I have an opinion as to that.

Q. And what is that opinion?

A. That certainly Mr. Smith is going to go ahead and commit other similar or same criminal acts if given the opportunity to do so.

Q. Now, Dr. Grigson, I believe you have stated that this man has no remorse or sorrow for what he has done?

A. No. He has none.

Grigson is always sure. He is difficult to cross-examine because of his certainty, even though much of what he says is scientifically questionable or purely speculative. When defense witnesses know he is to testify in the penalty trial, they can counter with their own psychiatrists who argue that the defendant is not likely to continue to be violent. Except, of course, it's hard to get a psychiatrist to be as certain as Grigson, since most psychiatrists are not convinced that their psychiatric licenses also qualify them to act as fortune-tellers.

As a result, Grigson is often asked no questions at all by the defense counsel. He has acknowledged that he thinks they are somewhat afraid of him and that doubtless pleases him.

After the jury returned with the death penalty in the *Smith* case, the decision was appealed. Smith went to prison in Huntsville, Texas, to wait out the months while the slow appeals process moved along. In 1976 the Texas Court of Criminal Appeals affirmed Smith's conviction and sentence, and in 1977 the U.S. Supreme Court refused to consider the case. Later in 1977 the U.S. District Court for Northern Texas agreed to hear the case and the judge vacated the death sentence on grounds that Smith's attorney had raised during the penalty phase of the trial—namely, that Grigson's failure to inform Smith or his lawyer that information gained during the competency hearing would be used during the trial was a violation of due process, of Smith's right to effective counsel, and of his right to introduce complete evidence. This was, of course, a victory for Smith, and Estelle, or rather the State of Texas (Estelle was the head of the Texas Department of Corrections against whom the original suit had been filed), requested a new trial, but that motion was denied.

Next, Texas-Estelle appealed the U.S. District Court's ruling to the U.S. Court of Appeals for the Fifth Circuit and, in 1979, five years after the original jury verdict, that court upheld the U.S. District Court's judgment for Smith. Texas was not about to give up so easily, however, and in 1980 the U.S. Supreme Court agreed to hear arguments and to make a final ruling on the case during its 1980–1981 season.

By 1981 Smith had spent seven years in the Huntsville prison. He had, so far, failed to live up to Dr. Grigson's billing of him as a man whose life would be dedicated to violence, unless one counted the fact that he had been knifed by another prisoner while at Huntsville. As Smith himself said, during his time in prison, the "only violent act [he'd] been involved in, [he] was the victim." During those seven years Dr. Grigson testified in many more cases in which the defendant stood a chance of execution. About one-third of the men awaiting execution in Texas prisons had had the "benefit" of Dr. Grigson's testimony. Also during those seven years, University of Texas Law Professor George Dix had begun seriously to study Dr. Grigson's testimony. In 1978 he published his study entitled "Participation by Mental Health Professionals in Capital Murder Sentencing." Dix was appalled by what he had found: Grigson was using a diagnostic category (sociopath) that the American Psychiatric Association had stopped using ten years earlier. Beyond that, Dix thought that the current evidence about psychiatrists' ability to predict violent behavior over the long-run conclusively disproved Grigson's views, and that Grigson's willingness to hinge these life-or-death judgments on a single ninety-minute interview was shocking.

Professor Dix had some considerable support on these issues, including the American Psychiatric Association. The APA is a national professional organization with 26,000 of the 33,000 psychiatrists in the United States as members, including Dr. Grigson. It is also the professional organization that sets the ethical standards for psychiatric practice and determines the officially sanctioned psychiatric diagnoses and mental illnesses. In the Smith case, the APA decided to file a legal brief in support of Smith and in opposition to its own member, Dr. Grigson. They filed their *amicus curiae* (friend of the court) brief with the Fifth Circuit Appellate Court, and when the U.S. Supreme Court agreed to hear *Estelle* v. *Smith,* they filed a second brief with that court.

The APA explained its willingness to be involved in the case by pointing out that it

> has monitored the administration of capital punishment statutes and the role of psychiatric testimony in that process. The instant case specifically involves the use of psychiatric testimony in Texas on the capital sentencing issue of whether a defendant is likely to commit criminal acts in the future. As such, it raises significant issues concerning the role of psychiatrists in capital cases. Resolution of those issues will have an important impact not only on the administration of capital punishment, but also on the quality and integrity of forensic psychiatry. . . . The Association is uniquely qualified to advise this Court as to the reliability of psychiatric predictions of long-term future criminal behavior, which is a key issue under the Texas capital sentencing statute. The Association is also qualified to discuss the potential impact of any restrictions as to such testimony on other criminal law issues concerning competency and sanity determinations. These factors are critically relevant to this Court's consideration of this case, and the American Psychiatric Association believes that they will not be adequately briefed either by petitioner or by respondent.

In its brief to the Supreme Court, the APA argued three major points. First, they argued that psychiatrists should be forbidden to testify in penalty phases of trials if their testimony was given with respect to predicting future dangerous behavior of the defendant. Second, they urged that if the court chose to permit psychiatrists to testify in the penalty phase of trials, it should require psychiatrists to give notice to the defendant that any statement he made in the interview could be used against him in the trial and that, further, he had the right to remain silent. Third, they urged that attorneys be given full notice of such examinations and of the possibility that testimony would be given as a result of the interview.

Although the APA chose to make its stand with *Estelle v. Smith*, its position applied to many more cases than this one. The use of psychiatric testimony in capital case-penalty trials was common in Texas and in several other states, with Virginia's procedures being most comparable to those of Texas. Grigson had proffered the same kind of testimony that the APA wanted outlawed in many Texas cases (eighteen of the Texas cases were specifically criticized by the U.S. District Court decision in *Estelle*). But, although Grigson figured prominently in these cases, he was not the only psychiatrist who was providing this kind of testimony. The APA was not apparently on a witch hunt against one of its own members. It did, however, seem to be in the unusual position of arguing that a limit should be placed on its own members' professional activities as a matter of principle. Even Jim Grigson didn't think they were out to get him, but he disagreed entirely with the APA's view of what principle was being defended in the case.

According to the APA, psychiatrists should not testify about probable future violence by defendants because scientifically conducted studies had repeatedly shown that psychiatrists had no particular expertise in making such predictions. In fact, some of the studies showed that psychiatrists were considerably less accurate than other groups, including policemen. Psychiatrists, it turned out, not only tended to overpredict dangerousness, expecting it a lot more frequently than it turned out to exist; they also tended to be fairly inaccurate in their selection as well. For example, suppose a group of one hundred people were to be evaluated for future dangerousness and the fact was that ten of them would actually be violent in the future. Psychiatrists might be likely to predict that twenty members of the group are dangerous (overprediction, since they have included at least ten "false positives," i.e., people who they say are dangerous but are not), and within that twenty that they have specified, only five of the actual dangerous groups of ten are included (thus, an inaccurate selection of 50 percent).

The APA claimed that, because there had been continuous requests for psychiatrists to make predictions about dangerousness both in civil and criminal matters, it had conducted a lengthy survey regarding violence and psychiatric understanding of "evaluation, management, and prediction of psychiatric behavior." The conclusion of the 1974 study was that psychiatrists had not been able successfully to predict violence at any high rate of reliability except in those instances where the individual had committed a significant number of violent acts over a period of time (for example, a parent who regularly abused a child). But, in those cases in which psychiatrists were fairly accurate, so were other people. It didn't appear that there was any psychiatric expertise that was required to make the prediction. College students had been able to predict it as well as psychiatrists. It was likely that jurors also could do it as well. It was probably a function of common sense.

The APA task force report concluded that "psychiatric expertise in the prediction of 'dangerousness' is not established and clinicians should avoid 'conclusory' judgments in this regard." It was just this kind of "conclusory" judgment that the APA particularly worried about in the testimony of psychiatrists like Grigson, for Grigson and others almost always testified that the defendant was certain to continue to be a danger to society. They spoke without doubts, without uncertainties, without any sense of probabilities in their judgments. The APA was convinced that psychiatry did not have this capability, and, if Grigson had it, it was not by virtue of his being a psychiatrist. They believed he should stop testifying under that heading, because it gave his views a dishonest cloak of greater expertise.

Many APA members, and particularly those involved in the preparation of the *amicus* briefs to the Appellate Court and the Supreme Court, were also appalled at other aspects of Grigson's testimony. But the nature of a legal brief is such that matters not specifically legal often are lost. As a result, the other serious objection about Grigson was cursorily mentioned in a footnote. What many psychiatrists found most outrageous about Grigson's behavior was his complete disregard for the authorized views of psychiatry, which were promulgated by the APA. In particular, they were offended by Grigson's repeated use in trial after trial of the term *sociopath*. Psychiatry had cast off that diagnosis in 1968. Grigson was, in effect, dragging up a part of their past they would just as soon forget.

To understand the importance of the sociopath issue, one must first understand something about how psychiatry, as a profession, developed. Early in the history of the field, psychiatrists were generally called alienists, a term borrowed from the French and indicating a specialist in diseases of the nervous system. "Psychiatrist" was a word the Germans used and it had unpleasant associations for Americans in the field because in Germany the term had heavy metaphysical associations, particularly relating to the soul or the mind (as opposed to the brain). These American doctors thought of themselves as scientists and as physicians to the body no less than other physicians, but physicians concerned with the nervous system. Around the turn of the century, however, there was a separation within the field and it was divided between two groups who became known as neurologists and psychiatrists. The neurologists took over the nervous system and the psychiatrists (no longer alienists) inherited "mental illness." The problem was, however, defining mental illness. No other medical specialist had ever had to face such a problem. With a fine sense of practicality and some sense of *hubris*, the psychiatrists decided that the only way to decide what was and was not a mental illness was for them to sit down and decide, which they did. The results were published in the first edition of the psychiatric blue print, the *Diagnostic and Statistical Manual*, or *DSM I*. This was published in 1952, drawing primarily upon the work of army psychiatrists during World War II. The American Psychiatric Association describes their initial effort as "the first official manual of mental disorders to contain a glossary of descriptions of the diagnostic categories." *DSM I* told practicing psychiatrists what was a mental disease and what was not (if it was not included, it was not a mental disease), what were the symptoms of particular diseases, and what were the prognoses. It was, in fact, a vitally important and extremely significant initial effort in classification and description of mental illness, but like any early work of that sort, it had many problems and errors. However, the problems that *DSM I* had were unlike the errors of other classification schemes.

Perhaps the diagnostic alteration best known to the public was the APA's decision that homosexuality was not a mental illness. Such an action seriously undercut public appreciation of psychiatry's positive work by suggesting that either psychiatrists' judgments were arbitrary or they had no standards at all. Americans were used to thinking of diseases as fixed entities. They could scarcely imagine doctors deciding that pneumonia, for example, wasn't a disease any more.

Reactions like these were related to the deeply ingrained connection and confusion between mental illness and sin. It was once widely believed that the mentally ill were in the devil's grip and many people still believe that, though their belief takes a somewhat altered form. Homosexuality, seen as a sin, had been caught up by psychiatrists as a mental disease. Then, when they decided that, if anything, it was merely a sin, they dropped it from their categories. From the public's point of view, it suggested that psychiatry thought homosexuality was neither sinful nor a mental illness. Psychiatry, on the other hand, was in the awkward position of having to renounce its belief in the mental illness part of homosexuality and at the same time divorce itself from religious or moral ideas about sinfulness. They didn't care what homosexuality was, as long as it wasn't considered a mental disease.

The story of sociopathy is not unlike that of homosexuality as *DSM I* evolved through *DSM II* and *DSM III*. Up until 1968 the APA included sociopath as a category of mental illness. Then, with the publication of *DSM II* in 1968, the term sociopath was dropped and a new classification, "antisocial personality disorder," was introduced. In *DSM III*, published in 1980, antisocial personality disorder continues to be listed as a mental illness and requires for diagnosis "a broad range of the patient's behavior." In the footnote in their brief in *Estelle*, the APA objected to Grigson's use of sociopath as a diagnosis because they don't use it any more, and even more so because his diagnosis was based on a brief examination in which the defendant evinced no remorse.

Grigson's use of the sociopath diagnosis as well as his willingness to be very certain about his judgments of future dangerousness are far more closely related to the idea of mental illness as sin than to the idea of mental illness as disease. And it is perhaps this aspect of his testimony that offended the APA the most.

Grigson, in fact, defended himself against his many critics as handily out of court as in. He finally began to refuse interviews to journalists, giving as his reason that he was tired of seeing himself referred to as "the hanging shrink," "Doctor Death," "the Doctor of Doom," and "the prosecution's hired gun." But in a 1978 interview with a reporter from a Texas magazine, Grigson allowed that the APA's disapproval of his actions was of little concern to him.

> I have been doing this since 1960, and in that time I've examined more murderers and more rapists than the combined number examined by the people who wrote the APA diagnostic manual. And based on my experience, here's *my* definition of a sociopath. First, a sociopath doesn't have a conscience. He feels no remorse about his crime. I say to him, "Hey, how did you feel about killing these people?" And he doesn't hang his head, his cheeks don't flush, he doesn't have any of the normal reactions you or I would have. Two, he repeatedly breaks the rules of society. Three, he cons and manipulates, lies, steals and cheats for the pleasure of it. Most of the district attorneys only prosecute a very specific type of person for these

> death cases. . . . If they prosecute a death case . . . then that guy has already been identified as bad, bad, bad. I think you could do away with the psychiatrist in these cases. Just take any man off the street, show him what the guy's done, and most of these things are so clear cut he would say the same things I do. But I think the jurors feel a little better when a psychiatrist says it—somebody that's supposed to know more than they know.*

Grigson suggests that he is willingly doing exactly what the APA is unwilling to have him do and is accusing him of doing: using the mantle of psychiatric authority to validate opinions that ordinary people would have anyway. But behind Grigson's words lies a more serious objection that the APA might have: that Grigson is using psychiatric authority to talk about sin, and that is really what Grigson is thinking of when he uses the term sociopath. Sociopaths are simply what a more religious culture knew to be unregenerate sinners, and they knew it with no less certainty than Jim Grigson knows it. And what could save a sinner? Not a psychiatrist, surely. That is why there is no treatment. Only God's grace can save a sinner, and grace is not a regular part of psychiatry or of prison rehabilitation.

Grigson is careful in defining the sociopath (or psychopath—he uses the terms interchangeably) to make sure that no one thinks that what he is talking about is a mental illness. If it were a mental illness, then perhaps some sympathy might appropriately be shown to the defendant. Furthermore, he counsels, a sociopath cannot be cured. The language begins to fall apart a little here, and the jury, unless they are totally spellbound by Grigson, might begin to wonder why something that isn't an illness even might be cured. But Grigson is simply covering all his bases. The defendant is not sick, cannot be cured, and will only get worse. If it were a riddle (what does a

* (*Texas Monthly Reporter*, "Killers and Shrinks," John Bloom, July 1978, pp. 64, 66, 68. Quote from p. 68.)

person have who is not sick, cannot be cured and will only get worse?), the only answer would be "sin."

It is perhaps this about Grigson that organized psychiatry hates the most. He drags psychiatrists backward into the semireligious quagmire from which they have struggled for so long to remove themselves. Grigson, on the other hand, thinks they're out to get him and others who testify as he does because he believes establishment psychiatrists want to eliminate the death penalty. If APA could prevent psychiatrists from testifying in the penalty phase of capital trials, jurors might be too soft-hearted to vote for the death penalty. Grigson is willing to testify because he believes in the death penalty and thinks that the small group at the APA that determines its public positions opposes him in order to oppose the death penalty.

The Supreme Court handed down its decision in *Estelle v. Smith* on May 18, 1981. The victory went to Smith. The APA got part of what it wanted, in that Grigson's style of witnessing was not approved. The Court ruled, first, that Smith's death sentence be vacated and a new penalty trial held. Second, in ruling on the procedures of the case, they held that psychiatrists may testify about future dangerousness where such testimony is permitted (an earlier Supreme Court decision on that question had pointed out that although such predictions were extremely difficult to make, someone, nevertheless, must make them). However, the court also ruled that the defendant must be informed of the purpose of any examination wherein his statements might later be used against him; that the defendant be permitted to invoke the Fifth Amendment; and that the defendant's lawyer be apprised of any such interview and testimony and have the opportunity to advise his client about answering questions.

Jim Grigson can continue to testify in the penalty phase of capital offense trials in Texas (or Idaho, Oklahoma, Virginia, Washington, or wherever else such testimony is allowed). He will have to tell the defendant the purpose of the interview and lawyers will doubtless urge their clients to be silent. Grigson will no longer be able to testify (as he has in the past) that the very refusal of defendants to answer a single question was evidence of their lack of remorse and of their severe sociopathy. Theoretically, if they will not speak to him, he cannot testify about them.

However, in at least one trial, Grigson had not interviewed the defendant but took the stand anyway. He was asked by the prosecution about a hypothetical case. "Suppose you interviewed a person who . . ." began the prosecuting attorney, who then proceeded to give a run down of the defendant's life. Grigson did not find any difficulty in making a judgment about this hypothetical person. He was a sociopath . . . extreme . . . no hope of change . . . only get worse. The defense attorney, on cross-examination, offered Grigson a second and different hypothetical case. Grigson listened, judged, and said yes, that hypothetical person was another sociopath, with no hope of change, and so on. The defense attorney then explained with subdued pleasure to Grigson and the jury, his hypothetical case was the life history to age nineteen of a well-known, very successful major league baseball player, Ron LeFlore.

Where there is no question of mental illness, there is no need for expert psychiatric witnesses. Doctors like Grigson provide us with excuses for not having to make decisions about capital punishment. To make such a decision is surely one of the hardest choices life can bring, but to make the decision on the basis of false premises or by hiding behind false expertise is immoral. If we cannot bear to make these decisions because they are so hard, then we should learn to get along without executions until we can accept the responsibility for the decision. Someone, says the Supreme Court, has to make these decisions. But it should not be Jim Grigson or psychiatrists; it should be us.

JOHN HINCKLEY

The Shooting of the President

TWO WEEKS AFTER A WASHINGTON, D.C., JURY FOUND John Hinckley not guilty by reason of insanity for the attempted assassination of President Reagan and the shooting of three other men, Hinckley sent a letter to a *New York Times* reporter. The letter purported to be the speech Hinckley would have made had the June 21, 1982, verdict been guilty, as many—perhaps including Hinckley himself—believed it would be. In the letter, he pointed out that "my actions on March 30, 1981, have given special meaning to my life and no amount of imprisonment or hospitalization can tarnish my historical deed." He continued, alluding to his long-distance infatuation with movie actress Jodie Foster, "I . . . committed the ultimate crime in hopes of winning the heart of a girl. It was an unprecedented demonstration of love. But does the American public appreciate what I've done?"

Love has frequently been the justification for deeds more disastrous and more far-ranging in consequences than an attempted presidential assassination, and thus we may disagree with Hinckley's description of his action as "unprecedented." Surely these are the words of a callow young man putting on airs. However, as to the American public's failure to appreciate his "historical deed," he is quite right. We did not appreciate it at all if by "appreciate" Hinckley means "approve." Nor did we appreciate thc jury's verdict of not guilty by reason of insanity. On the other hand, if "appreciate" is taken to mean "to understand," then perhaps the jury did appreciate Hinckley's historic act. And the American public appreciated the verdict. The jury's appreciation of Hinckley's act offered understanding infused with sympathy, while the public's appreciation of the verdict displayed understanding filled with alarm. A young man had shot the president and only by chance had not killed him. That he should be exonerated, and pronounced not guilty, when anyone could see him fire the gun time and time again on television replays, was itself some kind of crime and some perversion of justice. The American public fully appreciated the meaning of this verdict.

Thousands of letters have been written to newspapers and magazines since then, decrying the shamefulness and outrageousness of the verdict; accusing lawmakers, psychiatrists, and go-easy-on-criminals judges of making this travesty possible. And thousands of those letters have been considered important enough to be printed. Voters have bombarded legislatures across the country with requests to eliminate the insanity defense or to introduce a guilty but insane plea, and legislators have started to draw up new legislation. The U.S. Senate, in midsummer and at the height of the Washington, D.C., tourist season, was able to gear up for subcommittee hearings on federal insanity laws within days of the Hinckley verdict. If anything in this series of events was unprecedented, it was the speed with which these hearings were convened.

The public response suggested that John Hinckley had single-handedly created an immense new judicial problem. But the problems inherent in the insanity defense have been with us for a long time. For all of recorded history, we have been troubled by the question of mental illness and the mentally ill: who—and perhaps what—are they? How are we to regard them? To treat them? For more than a hundred years, the insanity defense has grown increasingly more incoherent as courts and legislatures have reinterpreted and broadened it to encompass diminished capacity, irresistible impulse, temporary insanity, and all the other causal descriptions of inexplicable actions. For more than fifty years, we have had the problem of the psychologizing of the public and of juries being ever more sympathetic to the deterministic, explanatory views of psychology. For the past thirty years the problem of psychiatric expert testimony has mushroomed because psychological theories have multiplied in number, complexity, and contradictions while psychiatric knowledge has grown at a snail's pace. For twenty years, we have had the problem of the successful insanity defense coupled with the use of modern psychotropic drugs that make it possible to release patients with mental disturbances who would once have faced life-long institutionalization.

The problems inherent in the insanity defense were made evident in the Hinckley trial:

1. The philosophical problem of allocating responsibility for human actions
2. The legal problem of defining states of mind that mitigate or eliminate imposition of moral guilt
3. The pyschological problem of jurors' identifying with the defendant, being unable to imagine how a fellow human could have performed certain acts unless he was crazy, and thus excusing and forgiving him
4. The medical problem of treatment that does not cure but can reduce symptoms so that imprisonment achieved under the name of institutionalization can no longer be justified because of civil rights.

The facts of the John Hinckley case are straightforward. The youngest child of a wealthy Colorado couple, Hinckley had been withdrawn and depressed for a number of years. His life had little consistent direction; he was in and out of college and periodically planned to go to Hollywood and become a musician. His family feared he was becoming dependent on Valium, which had been prescribed by a physician for anxiety. At his family's urging, John began seeing a psychiatrist who treated him with a combination of verbal therapy and behavior modification. The psychiatrist did not think the Valium was a problem, nor did he think Hinckley had a serious mental illness. He diagnosed Hinckley as an immature young man who needed help in establishing a life independent from his parents. The goal of the therapy was to get Hinckley out of his parent's home and into a job. Hinckley was never hospitalized for mental illness, nor had he ever been diagnosed as having any major mental illness.

During the months that this therapy took place, Hinckley was trailing back and forth across the United States, travels that were not known to the therapist. He wrote letters, poems, and short stories, frequently with violent and death-oriented themes. He pursued Jodie Foster, a student at Yale University, wrote her notes, called her on the phone, and, on the Yale campus, once asked her for directions.

By March 1981 John Hinckley had made an agreement with his parents and his therapist to get a job and move out of the family home. The plan didn't work. Hours after leaving a note at Jodie Foster's door, he called his father from New York and asked for help to get back to Colorado. His father reluctantly provided a plane ticket and John flew to Colorado. His parents gave him money, wished him well, but though they felt badly, told him that he could not return to the family home. The next word they had of him was the radio news a few weeks later that he had been arrested for attempting to assassinate the president of the United States.

In his writings, filled with fantasies and ramblings, Hinckley spoke of great events, his place in history, his death, his love for Jodie, and the death of others. He planned airplane hijackings and he wrote a short story about a young man who viciously murders his father. These are not the writings of the typical twenty-year-old. He had no friends and scarcely any acquaintances. His only girl friend turned out to be a story he had made up for his parents' benefit. His older brother and sister had not had much to do with him for years. Although he periodically planned a career as a musician, his parents had never heard him play or sing. He was a loner, he was alienated, he was insecure, he was confused. But was he responsible for his actions? Did he know what he was doing and that it was wrong?

It was established at the trial that Hinckley had purchased a handgun, had engaged in a considerable amount of target practice, and had been in suspicious proximity to both Reagan and Carter on several occasions prior to the shooting of President Reagan.

The philosophical question of the nature of individual responsibility permeates all aspects of John Hinckley's trial. Was it chance, for example, that he loaded his gun with the six devastator (exploding) bullets rather than with any of the relatively less damaging bullets that he possessed? Or did he intend to maximize injury? Was he infatuated with Jodie Foster or obsessed with Jodie Foster? Did his parents' unwillingness to let him come home in March 1981 inevitably lead him to the attempted killing, as Hinckley's father seemed to believe when, on the witness stand, he said it was all his fault? Almost every witness testified—either directly or indirectly—to two questions: Could he choose and did he choose?

Perhaps the most peculiar instance of this was the defense's contention that Hinckley's actions had been delineated and determined by the movie *Taxi Driver,* which starred Jodie Foster as a twelve-year-old prostitute. The movie's hero, Travis Bickel, is a taxi driver, a loner who is rejected by a girl, stalks a presidential candidate, and, to rescue the prostitute, shoots up a screenful of extras in a particularly blood-drenched scene. At the end of the movie, Bickel is seen as a hero. The defense contended that Hinckley had so identified with Travis Bickel that he had been obliged to reenact the events in his own life.

Surely there was a correlation. Hinckley had reportedly seen the movie fifteen times, although his devotion to Jodie Foster alone might account for that. He did stalk presidential candidates: testimony showed that he had tracked both Carter and Reagan at earlier times. He had certainly been rejected by his fantasy love, Jodie Foster. Although the climactic shooting of President Reagan and three others at the Washington Hilton could hardly be said to have rescued anybody from anything, it was sufficiently bloody and violent to be equal to the movie's conclusion. And, if the shooting did not make him a hero, it certainly made him famous. The defense convinced the judge that the parallels between the movie and Hinckley's actions were potentially meaningful, and the movie was shown to the jury during the trial, to make sure that they got the point.

But what, exactly, was the point? That life imitates art? Hardly news. That the immature are easily influenced? Yes, but that is a well-known fact and probably a normal and necessary stage in human development. How can we conclude an absence of personal responsibility from the fact that the young and inexperienced frequently model their lives on others who appear to be more in control?

Heroes and hero-worship were once an ordinary part of growing up. Young people were expected to idolize some figure—a parent or older sibling, a community or religious leader, a president or some historical personage. They dreamed about growing up and being like the hero. They imitated actions and laid out goals in conscious simulation of the hero's behavior, style, and achievements. It was a culturally endorsed and accepted way of growing up and finding direction. But the belief in heroes lost favor when the heroes whom the young chose no longer reflected the traditional values of adult society. When fast-living movie and television stars, or outrageous, rebellious musicians began to be the kind of people that the young looked up to as heroes, hero-worship seemed less appropriate. When their heroes were noble and good, we believed that such behavior on the part of the young was natural, wise, and virtuous. But when their heroes are bad do we believe that choosing such a hero is unwise and foolish, or do we now think that such choices are unnatural and crazy, the act of an insane person?

John Hinckley's defenders argued that he was beyond choice, that he was the captive of a bad hero. But the only evidence of his captivity is that the choice was a poor one. The reasoning seems to go like this: Travis Bickel is a bad person. No rational person would freely choose to model his life on the life of a bad person. John Hinckley modeled his life on Travis Bickel's. Therefore, John Hinckley is not a rational person. If we believe that rational people make only rational (or desirable) choices, then it is a short journey from that conclusion to a verdict of not guilty by reason of insanity.

At the trial, some of the testimony focused on whether Hinckley had planned the killing. The evidence is persuasive: he had purchased a gun and bullets, had learned how to shoot, and had found out where President Reagan was to be that day. He had taken himself and the gun and bullets to the Hilton at the appropriate time. He had written a note explaining how the "historical deed" would convince Jodie Foster of his sincerity. It is clear that John Hinckley had planned to shoot the president. In many insanity trials, the question of planning is central. In Dan White's trial, for example, there was much made about whether, when he pocketed his police revolver on the way to meet Mayor Moscone, the act proved planning or only proved that he often carried a gun. In this trial, there could be no such debate. Hinckley had surely planned the shooting.

But the defense lawyers bypassed the question of planning and premeditation by using the movie as the planning force. Not Hinckley at work here, they said. It was a movie script. No need for him to be responsible. No need for the movie maker to be responsible either, probably. Nobody was responsible. Following this line of thinking, a mind that is influenced by the outside world is a mind out of control and beyond responsibility.

There must be something about all this that is vaguely plausible since the jury bought the story. But if we were to change the events somewhat the foolishness of it becomes apparent. Suppose a lonely, misunderstood, isolated girl in Montana sees an extremely effective movie about a woman who gives up all the traditional rewards of life and instead works in miserable conditions, sacrificing her own health working with poor, abandoned children in some fetid city slum. And suppose the young girl is so impressed with the power and love that this woman has gathered unto her that she decides to emulate all the heroine's actions and goals.

If the young girl were to succeed and, as did Mother Theresa, eventually receive a Nobel Peace Prize, would the forensic psychiatrists of the world stand up and testify that she should receive no rewards for her deeds because she was not responsible for the good she had done? Would they swear under oath that she was merely under the sway of a powerful movie and that, when young and immature, her neurotic need for love and power had sent her in these directions?

We cannot have it both ways. It cannot be that good choices are our responsibility and bad choices are not. But the Hinckley defense argued that the good John Hinckley might have done was to his credit, while the evil belonged to something or someone else. And the jury agreed.

The legal problem of defining insanity was not limited to the usual questions in this trial. It is difficult enough to provide jurors with any precision about what the law means when it says that they must decide whether the defendant had, for example, the capacity or ability to understand that his contemplated act was wrong, or that he even had the capacity to contemplate the act. The problem of how much capacity or how much understanding is always present and essentially insoluble. But in this case, because it was tried under federal rules, there was an added problem. To obtain a guilty verdict, the prosecution had to prove that John Hinckley was sane and the legal standard of proof was "beyond a reasonable doubt." Federal courts require the prosecution to prove sanity; most states place the burden of proof on the defense, so that to gain an acquittal they must prove the defendant insane.

Burden and standard of proof are complex legal issues and many commentators on this trial have suggested that the jurors paid no attention to these issues because they did not understand what they meant. On the other hand, jurors were quoted as saying that they had handed down the verdict that the law required, implying that the legal constraints had forced them to make a decision of which they personally disapproved. But these statements might as easily be the result of the jurors attempting to absolve themselves of responsibility for a verdict that proved extremely unpopular.

It is, however, hard to imagine how any prosecutor could prove John Hinckley, or anyone else, for that matter, sane beyond a reasonable doubt. Sanity and insanity are, of course, legal, not psychiatric, terms. The law has been notoriously unsuccessful in defining insanity. It does not even attempt to define sanity. It is certainly not obvious that sanity is simply the absence of insanity, whatever that may be. A juror, representing the lay public, probably interprets insanity to be a condition of varying degrees, depending on the extent of abnormal behavior or the seriousness of the apparent mental illness. Thus, a defendant might evidence some small mental disorder or an extremely serious mental disorder, or be anywhere in between. Correspondingly, he might be somewhat insane or extremely insane, or anywhere in the middle. It is hard to imagine any defendant on trial for a serious crime who could not be seen as abnormal. The crime itself is abnormal behavior in the society, and to be a criminal is to be deviant. If he is abnormal and deviant, then he is surely also mentally disordered and thus at least somewhat insane.

Proving sanity is as difficult as proving good physical

health. A doctor can poke, prod, look, listen, and test to find illness but if he finds no evidence of it, he cannot be certain that the patient is well. There may be no detectable, empirical evidence of disease, but that does not prove the patient is well. Our knowledge of the body's functioning is not good enough for us to be able to assure "wellness." And our knowledge of the mind's functioning is microscopic compared to our knowledge of physical health. It is factually impossible to prove anyone sane or mentally healthy, although we might suppose they are sane unless proven otherwise, as is customary in most state courts.

When jurors are impaneled for a trial, the attorneys or judges often ask during the preliminary questioning whether the prospective juror understands what is meant by "preponderance of evidence" and "beyond reasonable doubt" standards of proof. They stress that the "beyond reasonable doubt" standard—which tends to prevail in criminal trials—means that no other reasonable explanation would account for the events that have transpired. They suggest that other explanations—irrational, fanciful, or far-fetched ones—are possible. But the jury need not be concerned with these. Only reasonable explanations need apply. By applying the "beyond reasonable doubt" standard of proof of sanity, the Hinckley jury was asked if there was any reasonable explanation for the assassination attempt other than the premeditated, thoughtful plan of a competent, rational human to kill President Reagan? The question must inevitably be answered affirmatively. That Hinckley was crazy is a reasonable explanation. That half a dozen or so psychiatrists and psychologists believed and testified that Hinckley was seriously mentally ill and incapable of controlling his actions certainly underscores the reasonableness of that explanation.

Placing the burden of proving sanity on the prosecution and then requiring that the standard of proof be "beyond a reasonable doubt" should have assured a not guilty by reason of insanity verdict for John Hinckley. The possibility that the jurors didn't understand burden and standard does not mitigate the law's foolishness for placing such a burden and standard. If one disinterested, qualified, expert forensic psychiatrist had testified to Hinckley's insanity, the prosecution could not have logically met the burden or standard of proof. And John Hinckley had enough peculiarities of mind and behavior that it was not difficult to find psychiatrists to testify to his incapacities, his confusion, his delusions, and his weakness.

The legal problem of the insanity defense in this trial was this: all the questionable mental states were placed in the not guilty by reason of insanity category. "If you are not absolutely sure of sanity," said the law, "rule insane."

"When in doubt," it counseled the jury, "make a finding of not guilty, even though you know the defendant committed the act. "When we speak of guilt," said the law, "we are talking about something else." We may well ask, exactly what is it that the law was talking about?

The expert witnesses in the Hinckley trial provided the usual panoply of conflicting definitions, variant diagnoses (four different kinds of schizophrenia from the defense alone), and wide-ranging role interpretations. Was killing Reagan an act of aggression toward Hinckley's father? Or was it identification with the Travis Bickel character? Was Jodie Foster an idealized mother or a fantasy child-princess in need of rescue? Was John spoiled and manipulating or helpless and driven?

As in the legal issues, this trial produced an unusual twist in the area of expertise when the defense sought to introduce the results of a CAT scan—a kind of X-ray of the brain using computerized axial tomography—to bolster the assertion that Hinckley was schizophrenic. It has been noted that the great weakness of the insanity defense (particularly from the defense's point of view) is its amorphousness. Unlike chemistry, pathology, or fingerprint expertise, psychiatric expertise tends to lack measurements, physical evidence, and quantifiable statements. When such evidence is available (for example, the machine-scored tests in Leonard Smith's second trial), juries seem very favorably disposed toward it and for good reason. After the vagaries of most psychiatric testimony —complicated sentences, judgments that need endless qualifications, abstract concepts defined in even less specific terms— numbers must seem a blessing. They can be counted, remembered, talked about, compared. Unfortunately, the numbers that psychiatric expertise occasionally provide only *appear* to be factual information. Under cross-examination or serious thought, they become as amorphous as the rest of the psychiatric testimony.

The Hinckley lawyers tried to introduce CAT scan results to provide genuine hard evidence—visual, physiological findings—to strengthen their contention that Hinckley had a serious mental disorder. The prosecution opposed the CAT scan results on the grounds that the scientific aspects of CAT scan technology would make the jury apply undue importance to the photos that showed shrunken brain tissue. They contended there was no evidence, either diagnostic or causal, to link reduced brain tissue to schizophrenia. Initially, the judge ruled the CAT scan evidence inadmissable. Later, he reversed his decision and permitted the testimony on the grounds that it might possibly be relevant.

This disputed testimony was a new but nonetheless typical example of the problem of psychiatric expert testimony. A jury of twelve very ordinary people were left to decide whether group A of highly trained medical specialists was correct in thinking that there was some relationship between Hinckley's brain quantity and his behavior, or whether group B of highly trained medical specialists was correct in saying that there was no known link between Hinckley's brain quantity and his behavior. Any sensible juror would surely wash his hands of the entire question. How could he possibly make such a decision? If experts are to be of use to jurors, they must bring them information, not more questions. If the doctors couldn't agree about CAT scans and schizophrenia, there is no reason to ask already burdened jurors to pass judgment on that dispute, too. They had their hands full already.

After the jurors announced the decision, there was the customary clamor by news media for inside information about what the jury really thought, how they really came to their decisions. The published accounts of the process certainly do not bolster one's faith in the jury system. But the trial did not bolster one's faith in the legal system or the psychiatric profession, either. Reports of jurors succumbing to pressure, anxiety, nervousness, and loneliness at being away from their families and reports of their willingness to vote certain ways in order to gain their own release from the ordeal all sound less noble, sincere, hard-working, and vigilant than we might have hoped. Posttrial interviews with jurors who allege they had always thought he was guilty but just didn't vote that way are a sad commentary on human weakness.

But these jurors also told enough about how they did make their decision to suggest that technical legal questions and technical medical questions were the last thing on their minds. They didn't talk to interviewers or Senate Committee members about shrunken brain tissue or burden and standard of proof. They talked about whether poetry was fact or fiction, they wondered why Hinckley didn't have any friends, and they puzzled over why he'd been traveling all over the country, spending money on fares and then not staying in any one place. They thought his ideas, writings, and behavior were weird. Their verdict seems to be an attempt to explain that weirdness.

The jurors seemed to focus on a narrow view of life, a view that seemed reasonable to them. John Hinckley certainly didn't seem reasonable to them. Here he was, writing all these poems and stories and letters that didn't make much sense. The defense psychiatrists had used Hinckley's bizarre writings as a basis for their diagnosis of severe mental illness and a prosecution psychiatrist had argued that such a practice was nonsense. "Poetry is fiction," he argued, and "a writer's writings are not that useful in determining the mental state of the writer." The jurors apparently took the question of whether or not poetry is true in a quite literal way. Did it actually represent Hinckley's true state of mind or had he just made it up, as a writer makes up the things he writes? This difficult question seemed to be resolvable by getting an official definition of poetry and, at one point, the jurors requested the judge's assistance in determining whether poetry was fiction or fact. The judge refused to provide a definition.

Although this conflict over the writings was surely only one of many issues the jury struggled with, most of their public comments have the same quality. When they could not understand on a personal level what Hinckley was doing or why he was doing it, they were inclined to see the behavior as evidence of mental illness and then of insanity. It wasn't natural not to have friends, said one juror. Another juror couldn't imagine why anyone would spend all that money on plane fares and then not stay put. That lack of understanding may evidence a man who knows how difficult money is to come by and how carefully it ought to be used. But John Hinckley obtained money easily and, if he had no sense of money, it was not because he was insane.

There are some suggestions in interviews with jurors that the group saw him as a young man who had everything going for him. The jurors—primarily lower middle class, blue-collar or clerical blacks living in Washington, D.C.—must have seen Hinckley as a privileged member of America's elite, which he was. There should be no excuse for his coming to such a bad end. He had everything. If someone with everything going for him has attempted to murder the president, then he must be crazy.

In the Washington, D.C., federal court where Hinckley was tried, those who are found not guilty by reason of insanity are sent to St. Elizabeth's Hospital and, after fifty days, the individual may request release in a court hearing. If he is found to be a danger to society no longer, he will be released. John Hinckley spent those fifty days in St. Elizabeth's undergoing yet further psychiatric evaluation. In spite of the hundreds of hours of examination prior to his trial—examinations that led to opposite conclusions by various psychiatrists—the St. Elizabeth's staff retested and made their decision. They did not, of course, have to decide whether he was legally insane; their job was simply to decide whether he continued to be a danger to himself or to others.

Hinckley's attorneys rushed to announce that they would not request his release until *they* were convinced that he was no longer a danger to society. This peculiar announcement suggested that they were somehow trying to apologize for having gotten Hinckley off and to demonstrate their basically responsible nature. But it is no concern of the courts whether Hinckley's lawyers (or his parents) thought he was dangerous. That expertise is the property of institutional psychiatrists. And the institutional psychiatrists concluded that he *was* dangerous.

Such a conclusion was likely, given public reaction to the verdict. But it is not always the case. When Robert Torsney was sent for evaluation, the institutional psychiatrists refused to be responsible for the courtroom conclusion and recommended Torsney's immediate release. In April 1982, just prior to the beginning of the Hinckley trial, Simon Karoly, who had threatened to kill the president, was released after he had been found not guilty by reason of insanity, in July 1981. The federal district court and the St. Elizabeth's psychiatrists believed that Mr. Karoly was no longer dangerous, although they released him with a diagnosis of paranoid schizophrenia. Psychiatrists were in a better position to recommend release in these less well-known instances. The Hinckley case, on the other hand, was a media event that led to widespread and severe criticism of both psychiatrists and psychiatry. Although many of the doctors who examined Hinckley before the trial believed he had no serious mental illness, the after-trial hysteria made a quick release most unlikely. What psychiatrist would want to be identified with that decision in the face of an enraged public?

Hinckley himself is reported to have said that if the psychiatrists concluded he was no longer dangerous, he was "going to walk out the door, whether the public likes it or not."

The public wouldn't have liked it. But even though he remains in St. Elizabeth's, he is eligible for review. Every six months the question of John Hinckley's dangerousness will be considered. Two weeks after he was returned to St. Elizabeth's, Hinckley sent the public a message about the insanity defense and his actions, speculating that "perhaps the uproar is for the belief that a person can shoot the President of the United States and not be punished for it." But, he counseled, the public should understand that "[s]ending a John Hinckley to a mental hospital instead of prison is the American Way." The American Way of what?

The long-term effects of the Hinckley trial are not difficult to imagine. The U.S. Senate subcommittee has held hearings and many notable lawyers and psychiatrists have been heard. After the Hinckley decision, nine bills were introduced in the House of Representatives and four in the Senate, adding to those that had already collected there to revise the insanity defense. President Reagan sent the Congress an "anti-crime package" that included reform, though not elimination, of the insanity defense.

At the state level, numerous proposals have been made, although no bill was rushed through in the months immediately following the Hinckley trial. But the impetus for revision clearly exists, and a number of states will probably adopt guilty but mentally ill pleas. Psychiatrists are conducting hand-wringing discussions in their professional newsletters about their role in the judicial process. The American Psychiatric Association will surely appoint a committee to study the question. Criminal lawyers have pointed out that the issue is being blown out of proportion because relatively few insanity pleas are successful. Eminent jurists have counseled caution, for "the principle behind the insanity defense . . . should not be abandoned thoughtlessly." Newspapers around the country received letters from mental health workers who made compassionate pleas for those seriously ill individuals who have no control over their actions, and from ordinary citizens who were angry at such misplaced compassion. Forensic psychiatrists who indulge themselves in this line of work continue to claim that they alone have the expertise to know whether or not they have expertise. The public will have difficulty knowing how to balance these claims against their own vital sense that something in all this is very wrong. After a while, they will forget the issue as it fades from the headlines. New laws will be in place, but the legal system will grind on inexorably in its customary way, allowing psychiatrists to testify to the same old vagaries but in the slightly different form required by new legislation.

One day, another case will spread across the newspapers and the public will again be outraged, unable to understand why there is still this problem.

"Didn't we get that straightened out after the Hinckley trial?" they will ask.

It will not be straightened out with quick-fix publicity appealing solutions. The guilty but insane and the guilty but mentally ill pleas are not panaceas for the problem, though they *sound* good. Untangling the puzzle will demand a broader and politically more difficult solution. Psychiatrists must not be allowed to testify to mental states but must testify to treatment possibilities. Jurors must not be allowed to make decisions about disposition without understanding whether treatment is possible or advisable. Decisions about guilt must be separated from decisions about disposition. The insanity defense must be eliminated to keep lawyers and juries from replacing responsibility for actions with explanations of behavior.

Conclusion

Criminal trials in which insanity is argued as a defense can and do often lead to injustice. This happens because (1) juries are asked to decide questions that predispose them to make arbitrary and emotional judgments because of either overidentification with or alienation from the defendant; (2) psychiatrists and other mental health professionals are encouraged to parade their opinions, guesses, and speculations under the banner of scientific expertise; and (3) society's views about criminality and craziness are so intertwined that an insanity defense to a crime does not make much sense.

In recent years increasing dissatisfaction has been expressed with the insanity defense and with the presence of psychiatrists as experts in the criminal courts. The defenders of the present system argue that the critics are wrong and that they do not understand how the insanity law and defense actually work. They argue that there are few insanity pleas, smaller numbers of insanity acquittals, minuscule abuses of the plea, and little stomach for it among judges, juries, lawyers, and defendants. The defenders of the system further assert that it is a humane, important, and effective plea, for it provides flexibility within the criminal justice system. Without it, they claim, real injustice would be done, for those who should not be held responsible for their actions would be treated like common criminals, with all the harshness that that implies.

The defenders are right in part. Insanity pleas do represent a small percentage of defenses in the criminal justice system and only about 25 percent of those defendants who argue for an insanity acquittal are successful. Perhaps only 1 or 2 percent of that group are actually released outright as a result of the acquittal. The statistics on these issues are not very reliable, but one study suggests that in 1978 about 3,500 people who were charged with either a felony or a misdemeanor were acquitted by reason of insanity. That would suggest that the insanity defense is offered in approximately 14,000 cases. Although the percentage may be small, as defenders of the plea contend, the actual number of cases and acquittals is considerable, as the critics charge. Furthermore, one can estimate that about fifty (1–2 percent) of these acquitted defendants were released without any treatment or hospitalization, and many more were released after only brief periods of treatment. A system that permits fifty or seventy or one hundred people to be freed despite their having committed an illegal act is not in itself intolerable. The problem is that the abnormal cases and the abuses, although small in number, receive disproportionate amounts of publicity and lead to public disrespect for both the courts and the psychiatric profession. A 1981 Associated Press–NBC News poll showed that 87 percent of the public think that too many murderers are not sent to jail because of insanity pleas, and 70 percent favored total elimination of the insanity defense.

A number of states have responded to this public concern by changing their laws. Montana has effectively eliminated the insanity defense and Idaho has specifically eliminated it. California has severely restricted its diminished capacity plea. Michigan, Illinois, Indiana, and Georgia now permit juries to find a defendant guilty but mentally ill. More than twenty other states are considering adding the guilty but mentally ill plea to their systems. These reforms have proved politically popular because they respond to people's heightened fear of crime and their concern that the courts are releasing criminals too easily and too quickly.

Unfortunately, reform measures that are easily and quickly passed are usually reforms that change nothing. In the states where action has been taken, there are reports that things are very much the same as before, although the names of things may have changed. The new guilty but mentally ill plea has all the attendant problems of the old not guilty by reason of insanity plea. When psychiatrists are not allowed to testify about whether or not the defendant actually understood what he was doing, they begin to testify about whether he had the capacity to understand what he was doing. If that is forbidden, they start testifying about whether he had the capacity to intend harm. The focus of their testimony changes slightly, but the testimony is no more precise, no less misleading, and no more likely to avoid injustice.

In order to make any difference, it will not suffice to make minor changes. Such an approach might please the public in the short run, but it will disappoint them in the medium run and increase their cynicism about government and institutions in the long run. If the insanity plea is to be reformed, changes must be broad and many people who make their living by the current procedures will have to be offended. Criminal defense attorneys and forensic psychiatrists in particular will oppose reform because their interests are going to be injured by real change.

The need for reform is not based on the public's misperception of the number of cases in which the insanity plea leads to injustice. The need for reform flows instead from the qualitative and symbolic significance of the real abuses that do occur. The seven cases in this book illustrate the kind of abuses that the use of the insanity plea can entail. This chapter proposes a broad outline for the kind of reform that would be effective and honest. It advocates (1) an elimination of the insanity defense, (2) the elimination of most psychiatric testimony, including all testimony by psychiatrists about the defendant's state of mind, (3) the adoption of the guilty but mentally ill plea, and (4) the separation of guilt and penalty phases of a trial when the defendant pleads mental illness. All four changes would be necessary for the system to provide any real improvement.

These seven cases are not presented as representative of the insanity defense cases submitted to jurors throughout the United States. Instead, each has been chosen because it represents one aspect of the problems inherent in the insanity defense.

The case of Dan White shows how psychiatrists play upon jurors' emotions by offering testimony that explains behavior in compassionate psychobiographical form and provides an excuse for reduced responsibility.

The Poddar case shows the ability of the judiciary to use technical points of law to overturn jury verdicts when their assessment of the defendant's mental state differs from the jury's opinion.

The case of Leonard Smith shows how the jurors' sympathies can be attracted by a defendant and how mental health experts can provide an apparently scientific base for the jury to use as an acceptable rationale for an otherwise unacceptable decision.

The Tex Watson trial demonstrates the disarray, vagueness, and confused, conflicting opinions of psychiatrists.

The case of Robert Torsney demonstrates the error of trying to use involuntary treatment as an alternative to punishment.

The case of Benjamin Smith exemplifies the problem of psychiatric testimony, even if insanity is not at issue, when psychiatrists become advocates for specific decisions, using the cloak of their medical authority in the absence of any expert information on the topic at hand.

The case of John Hinckley shows how jury members are manipulated not only by psychiatrists but also by one another. In the midst of the public outcry about the decision, those jurors who spoke to the press were almost incoherent in their attempts to explain the outcome. After the fact, they didn't seem to *know* why they voted not guilty by reason of insanity.

These problems do not appear in every case in which the insanity defense is claimed, but they are potential problems every time the plea is considered. The "psychologizing" of American culture continues to expand, and we are all readier to understand and explain behavior than we are to judge it. As a result, with the passage of time, more jurors will be responsive to the kinds of insanity defenses that these cases represent. We are already seeing an overrepresentation of policemen who kill and of women who have killed their husbands or children among those who are found not guilty by reason of insanity. With both these groups, jurors are likely to find insanity because what else would explain such an act? We are less likely to think that perhaps some policemen, some wives, and some mothers may be undisciplined, immature people who have failed to exercise self-control and who injure or kill others because that is what, in the moment, they unreflectively choose to do. Idealizations of friendly policemen, loving mothers, and helping wives are strongly ingrained in our minds. When psychiatrists give us apparently scientific reasons to explain violent acts, we grab hold of the explanations. Any explanation that conforms to our prior ideas is more acceptable than one that will require us to rethink our version of what the world is like. In insanity defenses, psychiatrists often act to buttress our fanciful and kindly visions of reality. A great fault of psychiatric expert witnesses is that under the guise of telling us truths about human responsibility, they give us explanations of behavior and histories of character development. By doing this, they allow us, when it suits our purposes, to forgive the guilty and even to let them go free. What suits our purposes is a defendant whose past we can understand as normal and whose future does not fill us with fear because he does not seem to be likely to repeat his violence. We acquit by reason of insanity someone whose past and future are pretty much like our own, but whose present is unexpectedly clouded by a violent act that psychiatrists are willing to explain away.

If jurors cannot identify with the defendant, he is unlikely to be found not guilty by reason of insanity. From the jurors' viewpoint, the difference between insanity acquittals and guilty verdicts is the difference between hospitalization and imprisonment. If we feel sympathy for a defendant, we hospitalize him. If we feel alienated from or frightened by the defendant, we imprison him.

We choose hospitalization because we believe that hospitals are not punitive. The hospital will provide the unfortunate defendant with treatment so that he need never again fall into such a difficult position. Furthermore, the psychiatrists who explained why the defendant should not be held responsible for the crime are members of the same profession as those doctors who will help restore the defendant to a proper life. Finally, the jurors trust the psychiatrists not to release the defendants until they have cured them.

It is a simple paradigm. It's a story, a cultural myth, a fairy tale about how there are some really bad people and some really good people. We are the really good people but sometimes we good people do bad things. But when that happens, we don't become *bad* people. Really bad people break the law and go to prison and are punished. Good people who do bad things shouldn't be punished the way really bad people are punished. They should be helped not to do bad things again. Doctors can treat them.

How do you tell really bad people from good people who do bad things? Easy; really bad people aren't like us. They're hippies, drug addicts, criminals, foreigners, or street people. It's easy to see who is really different. The fact that psychiatrists do not know how to cure the good people any more than penologists know how to rehabilitate the bad people is beside the point. What counts is the jury's (and our own) fantasy about what is going to happen. In the Leonard Smith trial, for example, the jurors believed that Smith would spend a long time in a mental hospital. That was their safety net, and it permitted them to be compassionate toward Smith and to acquit him of the murder of Lyman Bostock. They had no reason to believe in this long-time hospital stay that they projected. No evidence was given about it, and no one even speculated about what psychiatry could do for Leonard Smith. But their belief in how it ought to be overrode the fact that they had no information about Smith's future in a mental hospital. Jurors base their decisions on their own "expert" opinions about human behavior and on their own fantasies about how the world works. Then they use psychiatric speculations given as testimony to shore up their judgment. It's shoddy construction.

But what does this have to do with the insanity defense itself? What does it have to do with craziness? Even if we were able to eliminate the abuses of the insanity defense that stem from the excess compassion and myth-making of juries, and from psychiatric speculation in the cloth of expertise, we would still be left with the problem of the insanity defense itself. If the insanity defense is a legitimate one, we must be able to make some genuine distinctions between criminality and craziness. They cannot simply be two words that express our potential degree of sympathy or disapproval for the deviant behavior of others.

Although we make legal and philosophical distinctions between criminal and crazy behavior, do we in actuality see them as different? If there is a distinction between them, it frequently blurs, both in our thoughts and in our actions. We think of them as different in terms of responsibility, but we also think that craziness is "wrong" in much the same way that we think crime is wrong. Certainly we are, in practice (as opposed to in the courtroom), as uncomfortable with and fearful of the mentally ill as we are of and with the convicted criminal.

When we talk about mental illness we are for the most part talking about behavior that is abnormal and deviates from whatever the culture finds acceptable. Criminal activities are also culturally defined as abnormal behavior. Certainly there is no objective standard, measurement, or microscopic analysis that marks a clear difference between them. We are comfortable thinking about these two categories as different forms of behavior because that is what one part of our culture has taught us to do, but we usually act as if they were the same and we are equally comfortable with that view. This produces tension in our attempts to formulate policies for either group.

Today deviant behavior—criminal and crazy—is being increasingly medicalized, that is, scientists are attempting to find physiological causes for various types of behavior, ranging from violence to schizophrenia to alcoholism. The characterization of deviant behavior as illness rather than as personal choice or as character demonstration is new. There is a remarkable irony in this because, at the same time, we are seeing a growing belief that physical illnesses (ranging from cancer and heart attacks to the common cold) are the results of individual choices about life-styles and peoples' willingness to learn adequate coping techniques. Thus, deviant behavior —whether it is crime or craziness—is coming to be seen as entirely physiological; deviant physiology—that is, sickness— is beginning to be seen as the result of character defects or learning flaws. Samuel Butler foresaw this strange reversal more than a hundred years ago when, in the satiric novel *Erewhon*, he created a society in which embezzlers were sent to the hospital to receive sympathetic professional treatment, as well as flowers, cards, candy, and visits from their understanding friends; and tuberculars were sent to prison and forever stigmatized for choosing to engage in such loathesome antisocial behavior.

We have not yet fully endorsed the *Erewhon* view of crime and illness, but we are suffering some comparable problem when, with the insanity defense, we have to decide whether it is criminality or craziness that is before us. In theory, we frown on criminality but extend our compassion to craziness, so it is important to think about how we distinguish them.

Some have suggested that the mentally ill differ from the criminal in that crazy behavior is idiosyncratic and not easily generalized, whereas criminal behavior is defined in terms of its common elements (theft, burglary, homicide, etc.). But, in fact, the Diagnostic and Statistical Manual of Mental Disorders does exactly that. Schizophrenic disorders and paranoid disorders are just as much generalized categories as are thefts and burglaries; psychotic (disturbed reality testing) and neurotic (intact reality testing) disorders are comparable, as categories, to felonies and misdemeanors.

Others have suggested that a critical difference between the two is that much—if not all—of mental illness is characterized by deviant or abnormal thoughts, whereas crime is typically determined by deviant actions. Yet the thoughts of criminals may be fully as deviant as those of the mentally ill. When bank robber Willy Sutton was asked why he robbed banks, he replied, "Because that's where the money is." Although startling and amusing in its simplicity, the reply does not exactly demonstrate "normal" thinking about the relationship between banks, money, and people. Finally, it is not the deviant thoughts of crazy people that bother us most. It is that they insist on believing in them and acting upon their beliefs. We would find them more tolerable if they would just *think* deviantly and *act* normally.

Some people have suggested that criminal behavior is more offensive than crazy behavior. The mentally ill sometimes commit criminal acts, but the acts of the mentally ill that are not criminal, acts that are simply crazy behavior, are not necessarily different from the acts that we define as criminal. Both offend, create fear, or in some way harm others, but mentally ill behavior is less offensive in degree. However offensive the crazy act is, it is not offensive enough to be made a crime. If so, criminal behavior is serious, crazy behavior; crazy behavior is mild criminality. Even if this distinction holds, it is a culturally defined one. It is not a difference that is inherent in the categories themselves.

Our attitudes toward the mentally ill and toward criminals are remarkably similar, considering how differently we think we characterize them. Both mental patients and criminals are ostracized, imprisoned, and stigmatized in the United States because they do things that frighten other people. Both the insane and the criminal are deprived of their freedom and may have difficulty obtaining their release from a prison or hospital. If they are released, they are likely to find it difficult to locate housing or gain employment. We do not welcome the ex-criminal or the ex-mental patient into our lives, for each has crossed an invisible line that makes them different and, to our primitive thinking, therefore dangerous. Despite these powerful feelings of exclusion, our official societal position is that having paid their debt, both criminals and the mentally ill belong to society as much as everyone else. This view is expressed through the courts and social service organizations. The courts frequently make decisions that focus on the protection of individual rights and assert that the mentally ill and the alleged criminal are both as much persons under the protection of the Constitution as are the sane and the law abiding. Social service agencies also conduct small but steady campaigns to urge society to accept former criminals and mental patients back into the flow of our lives. Each, they argue, has paid for his sins: prison for the criminal, hospitalization and treatment for the mentally ill. Nonetheless, we shun the criminals and the crazies. We shut them out because they are different from us. We offer treatment or rehabilitation to them, but it is not very successful since the recidivism rate is very high. Perhaps they are forever different because we forever think of them as different. Perhaps they just *are* different, but it is that difference that criminals and crazies have in common that holds our minds most strongly and makes it confusing for us to sort out the relationship between criminality and mental illness.

Criminality and craziness are, as far as we know, matters of external and, to some extent, arbitrary definitions. When behavior is described as a continuum, both are at the far end and both are clearly deviant. Some day we may have more knowledge and a better understanding, but we do not have it yet. As a result, we need to think seriously about why we should choose to treat the mentally ill differently from others when their behavior is criminal. We need to think about whether there should even be an insanity defense.

Some believe that mental illness itself makes the individual incompetent and that all his actions are a product of the illness. We might feel comfortable with that if, by mental illness, we meant only the behavior at the very extreme end of the spectrum, for example, the floridly delusional psychotic or the trancelike catatonic. It is this group that the law had in mind when the insanity plea was accepted as a legitimate defense to criminal responsibility. Now we see mental illness and incipient insanity everywhere.

In an earlier time, people lived in a more heterogeneous environment, were far more accustomed to a wide range of human behavior and, as a result, recognized the far end of the spectrum when they saw it as insanity. The homogenization of America in this century and the conformity created by television and other mass media have resulted in people living far more similar lives now than they did previously, in experiencing a much narrower range of behavior, and, consequently, in defining acceptable or normal behavior very narrowly. As a result, they apply the term "insane" to a much broader range of human experience. It apparently covers Dan White's anger, Leonard Smith's frustration, Prosenjit Poddar's longing desire, and Robert Torsney's fearfulness. These men bore little or no criminal responsibility for their emotions, and by giving them lesser verdicts or freedom, we are perhaps suggesting that like them, if we lose our control, we will not have to be held accountable for our actions.

When jurors are asked to make these decisions, they bring to the task their own personal biases. Jurors, however, do not have to reveal these biases because they can reach a verdict on the basis of the testimony of psychiatric experts who are presumed to know what they are talking about. On the other hand, jurors are sometimes hostile toward certain psychiatrists and they can doubt their expertise. In addition, individual psychiatrists, as well as health professional societies, have gone on record with their belief that psychiatrists have no special knowledge to contribute to the guilt phase of a criminal trial. Karl Menninger, one of America's best-known psychiatrists, has written that psychiatrists ought never to be allowed to testify in courtrooms. Certainly in the Torsney case the New York State Department of Mental Hygiene psychiatrists looked down their noses at the contribution of forensic psychiatrists, and they criticized forensic psychiatrists in general as well, urging that they not be permitted to testify as experts in criminal trials. The American Psychiatric Association has also opposed the use of psychiatrists in some phases of the criminal process.

A recent article by the director of a forensic psychiatry training center concedes that the origins and the categories of mental illness have not been scientifically validated and that clinical opinions reflect a high degree of uncertainty. Despite this, he argues that such testimony is better than "mere speculation," which may be true. The question is, why should we want to allow such influential testimony when its major claim is that it is better than guessing? If we cannot have better than that, we should do without.

Jim Grigson pointed out in one of his interviews that his expertise only gives the jurors a respectable reason to do whatever it is they wanted to do in the first place. He further acknowledged that his expertise on these occasions is pretty much composed of common sense. If that is what is going on, then the system's use of psychiatrists is morally bankrupt.

In cases where the defendant successfully maintains an insanity defense, he is not held accountable, and, therefore, the psychiatrist who has testified to the defendant's mental incapacities need not consider himself responsible for the outcome, since the jury makes the decision about the verdict and the psychiatrist has only offered his opinion. The jury does not need to feel responsible for the outcome either, because it has been obliged to take into account the scientific opinion of the doctors. As it turns out, no one has to feel responsible for the crime, the victim of the crime, or the criminal's release. Everyone can point to someone else as being responsible for whatever happens.

It is an ideal arrangement for ensuring that, sometimes, the guilty will go free when we are too sympathetic to certain kinds of violence, too blind to our own hidden and hostile natures, too frightened of madness to face up to it, too anxious to be compassionate toward those with whom we can identify, and too irresponsible to make our own decisions. From this complex set of feelings, we create a need for the psychiatric expert in criminal trials, but his presence creates more problems for us than it solves.

It is not psychiatry or psychiatrists alone who are at the center of this problem. The law permits all this and even encourages it. The adversary system, which may well be an admirable method for ferreting out the "truth" of factual matters, is a poor vehicle for trying to understand and evaluate the complexities of the human mind. Since 1843, when the British judiciary took on the insanity issue with the M'Naghten case, courts have had to contend with this problem. For more than a hundred years, the M'Naghten rule prevailed as the standard in all American courts. It states that:

> At the time of the committing of the act, the party accused was labouring under such a defect of reason, from disease of the mind, as not to know the nature and quality of the act he was doing; or, if he did know it, that he did not know he was doing what was wrong.

In 1954 a Washington, D.C., circuit court decision announced a new standard for determining a defendant's criminal responsibility. This, the short-lived Durham rule, specified that "an accused is not criminally responsible if his unlawful act was the product of mental disease or defect." In the District of Columbia thirty-four acquittals on the basis of not guilty by reason of insanity had been given during the four years previous to the application of the Durham rule. In the four years after Durham was held to be the proper standard, the number of acquittals from insanity pleas rose to one hundred and fifty. The liberal Durham rule fell rapidly into disfavor with this increase and in 1972 was repudiated in the District of Columbia, although a version of it continues to be the legal standard in New Hampshire.

It must also be remembered that an acquittal on the basis of an insanity plea in 1954, when the Durham rule was announced, amounted to a lifetime sentence in a mental hospital or a hospital for the criminally insane. Psychiatry had little to offer other than long-time custodial care for the patient who was genuinely mentally ill. But the discovery of psychotropic medications and their rapid, widespread use in mental hospitals changed all that. By the mid-1960s the populations of mental hospitals were flowing back into the towns and cities that had cast them out. For the most part, these patients had not been cured with the new medications, but their symptoms—which were often disabling to the patients and threatening to others—could be brought under control. Although these former patients might still be considered mentally ill, medication made it possible for them to exist in the community.

Psychotropic drugs changed mental hospitals from snake

pits and permanent holding tanks to places where the idea of releasing patients was both possible and probable. If there tended to be a revolving-door existence for many patients, with repeated admissions and releases, who would question that an in-and-out patienthood was better than permanent disposal in the back wards?

The possibility of release applied equally to those patients imprisoned in the hospitals by the courts as a result of insanity acquittals. Some of them could be treated with the new drugs and released in a relatively short time. The simplicity of the Durham rule and the effectiveness of psychotropic medications created a situation that resulted in the rapid demise of Durham.

The next attack on the M'Naghten rule was by the American Law Institute. It stated:

> 1. A person is not responsible for criminal conduct if at the time of such conduct as a result of mental disease or defect he lacks substantial capacity either to appreciate the criminality of his conduct or to conform his conduct to the requirements of law.
>
> 2. The terms "mental disease or defect" do not include an abnormality manifested only by repeated criminal or otherwise antisocial conduct.

This definition was eventually adopted by twenty-eight states as a replacement for M'Naghten. Most of the remaining states still use M'Naghten, sometimes in combination with "irresistible impulse" or "diminished capacity" tests. It was the diminished capacity rule that permitted Dan White to receive a light verdict, for the point of diminished capacity is to permit a jury to find guilt for a lesser offense, for example, finding for manslaughter in what would otherwise appear to be first- or second-degree murder. Diminished capacity pleas permit juries to have some discretion in those cases where full insanity cannot be found but where there are mitigating factors that flow from the accused's mental state.

A recent case in which diminished capacity might have made sense involved a battered wife who had been abused by her husband for a number of years. One night, after a particularly harrowing encounter with him, she finally packed her children in the family car, set fire to the house in which her husband slept, and, in a daze, drove to the police station. Such a case is perhaps what legislators had in mind when they established the diminished capacity plea. In this instance, the prior history of abuse and the wife's great terror of her husband might be said to have diminished her capacity to "conform her conduct to the requirements of the law." However, she was found *not guilty by reason of insanity* and was released. It is true that Michigan had no diminished capacity plea, but surely one can legitimately ask whether insanity was the proper ruling in her case.

Murdering a spouse is offensive to society even if the spouse is a despicable person. The point of the law is to keep individuals from making those kinds of judgments, and the need for law derives from the human inclination to make such judgments in the heat of emotion and in stressful situations. It is absurd to claim that stress and emotion excuse criminal acts, for they are the reasons for the law's necessity. If being a battered wife is an indication of a mental illness (as some psychiatrists claim it is), and one so severe that it should eliminate criminal responsibility (as the defense psychiatrists in this case successfully argued), or diminish criminal responsibility (as psychiatrists in California might have argued), then surely the appropriate response is neither freedom nor less time in prison than conviction for the crime would ordinarily receive. The appropriate response is punishment and treatment.

Through M'Naghten, Durham, the American Law Institute, and such terms as irresistible impulse and diminished capacity, we have tried again and again to find some way to describe, define, and justly handle the situations at the intersections of criminality and craziness. The results of our attempts give poor testimony to our success. Psychotic delusional killers (Mark David Chapman, who killed John Lennon, is a recent example) go to jail forever, but people like Robert Torsney, Leonard Smith, Prosenjit Poddar, and the abused wife—all under emotional stress when they committed their murderous acts—go free. Is this what we mean to say about our feelings toward the mentally ill?

What happens when a defendant is acquitted on an insanity defense? The original point of the successful insanity plea was to change the locale where the legally not-guilty (but factually guilty) defendant served his time. Instead of being guilty-in-prison for a long time, the defendant with an insanity acquittal could be guilty-in-a-mental-hospital forever. Such a choice would, presumably, find few takers in a day when prisons and mental hospitals were equally repressive and barely distinguishable in their physical settings and psychological tones. Both were, in fact, punishment and imprisonment. Today, when many mental hospitals have been upgraded beyond most prisons and are committed to releasing patients as soon as possible, an insanity acquittal may be more appealing than a prison sentence, and it is certainly preferable to either a life sentence or a death sentence. For some, the possibility of serving little or no time for a real crime is genuinely there, as the case studies in this book point out, and criminal lawyers know it is possible.

In most states, a defendant who is acquitted by reason of insanity does not receive an automatic commitment to a mental institution. Many jurors think an insanity verdict means that the defendant will be hospitalized for a long time, but that is simply no longer the case. Mental illness is often an on-again, off-again matter. If the defendant were floridly psychotic, he would probably not even have stood trial, since the law requires him to be sufficiently competent to understand the proceedings and to assist his attorney. In cases where the crime was a result of an unlikely or unrepeatable series of events, such as the wife who had been abused for many years or Dan White's betrayal by the mayor, acquittal may lead to immediate release, because there is little prospect of danger from these persons. Had Dan White been found not guilty by reason of insanity, he probably would not have been considered dangerous to others. Thus it is unlikely that he would have been held in a mental hospital for any longer than was required to evaluate his condition.

In many states the critical question is whether or not the individual is dangerous to others in society. If he is not guilty of any criminal offense, and if he poses no threat to others, what right or rationale does society have to deprive him of his liberty by imprisoning him? The defendants cited in this book could probably have used some of the help that psychiatry says it has to offer, but in most states, the mentally ill cannot be compelled to accept this help if they are not dangerous to themselves or to others. If the defendant is not dangerous at the time of the verdict, he cannot be committed involuntarily to a psychiatric hospital or, in most states, cannot be ordered to undergo outpatient treatment.

It is clear that juries often do not understand the implications of their decisions. This is not surprising since the law as it relates to mental illness is complex and confusing and jurors are unlikely to understand the nuances of the laws relating to involuntary mental commitment. Moreover, the laws require jurors in criminal cases to be kept in ignorance about the consequences of their decisions. The lengthy judicial decisions in the Torsney case express the frustration of those who do understand this law. The attempt to find some way to hold Torsney was impressive but it was in the long run unsuccessful.

Given that there are substantial problems with this confluence of jurors, law, and psychiatry, what alternatives are possible? What could we do that would be better? We could, of course, do nothing and hope that psychiatry and science would make a dramatic, technological or medical breakthrough that would permit mental illness to be wiped out just as polio was. As appealing as this solution is, its likelihood is improbable.

The chief value of the current system of not guilty by reason of insanity with psychiatric expert testimony is that it acknowledges our intuitive feeling that guilt requires responsibility and that the genuinely insane person (i.e., those at the far end of the spectrum) is not responsible for his or her actions. Their thoughts and perceptions are so distorted that we cannot reasonably expect them even to understand the rules of the game that the rest of us are playing. This group may need to be accommodated in some special way in order to protect themselves and others, but being declared legally guilty is the least of their problems.

Another so-called "benefit" of the current system is the diffusion of responsibility. By permitting expert mental health testimony in an adversarial context, the responsibility for making very difficult and often personally burdensome decisions about guilt of the marginally sane/insane person is diffused, and the weight of the decision is thereby lightened. It is asking a great deal of jurors to require them to agree to a verdict that may result in death by execution. To ask such a decision when the defendant shows marginal signs of insanity is even more awesome. The size of the jury itself diffuses some responsibility, but each one is known to have agreed. The introduction of expert mental health witnesses may be comparable to the introduction of blank cartridges in the rifles of firing squads. No one need be quite sure who did the fatal act.

The greatest drawback of the current system is that the existence of the not guilty by reason of insanity plea can encourage a lawyer with a sympathetic, out-of-control defendant to use the plea. Wanting the best outcome for a client, a criminal lawyer may use the insanity plea. Sometimes it works, but when it is only a gambit or a ruse, the sense and sensibilities of the public are offended, and respect for both the courts and the psychiatrists is reduced.

The ideal revision of the current system would permit jurors to take their roles and their decisions seriously, without being so burdened with complex theories that they suffer intellectual or emotional paralysis, thus increasing the incidence of hung juries. In addition, a revised system would reduce the likelihood of insanity pleas being "used" to get a person off but would permit some kind of separate handling for those who need special consideration because of their extremely deviant perceptions and thought processes. However, it may be logically impossible to maintain the insanity defense for the benefit of the seriously mentally ill and not have it susceptible to abuse by the neurotics and impulsives with sympathetic life stories.

Some argue that a defendant has both a legal and a moral right to psychiatric testimony. However, the legal right presupposes the existence of the insanity defense. If it were eliminated, as it has been in some states, no such legal right need exist. The moral issue, in fact, is the more important one. Is it fair to deprive a defendant of a psychiatrist's expert testimony with respect to the defendant's state of mind? It is unfair only if the psychiatrist actually knows something about the defendant's mental condition at the time the criminal act was committed. Since he does not, his testimony is no more obligatory than that of anyone else who tries to explain past behavior in terms of mental states.

Psychiatry cannot help us in these cases because its practitioners still know too little. They cannot tell us much about the specific state of the defendant's mind and certainly cannot tell us anything definite about the relationship between his state of mind and the criminal act he performed. The law has failed equally in its attempts to define the terms it thinks relevant and necessary to make reasonable dispositions in these cases.

Many have argued that the restriction or elimination of

psychiatric testimony would bring new reasonableness into court proceedings. But others have suggested that the real problem is the adversary setting of psychiatric testimony. This could be eliminated if the court appointed its own experts for testimony. There would no longer be "defense" psychiatrists and "prosecution" psychiatrists. But how would these court psychiatrists be chosen? Would permitting the court to choose them or having them chosen randomly reduce the likelihood that they would have different opinions as to whether or not the defendant was capable of harboring, or did harbor, the requisite state of mind? Such a conclusion is only possible if one believes that the psychiatrists who currently testify would say anything for a price. But it is not the adversary system that creates different opinions among psychiatrists (although it perhaps does exaggerate the differences). It is that psychiatrists do not agree and do not have a sufficiently common view of what mental illness is and how it is defined. Psychiatrists appointed by the court would have no corner on "truth."

If the jury is capable of deciding issues of fact as they relate to points of law, perhaps they also can decide issues of fact as they relate to points of psychiatry. The jury currently decides what crime has been committed as well as whether the defendant has committed it. They make this decision in the light of the evidence and the court's instructions. If they are also to decide about the defendant's mental state, then perhaps they also need some kind of instruction about how to interpret psychiatry. An official court psychiatrist could give the jury psychiatric instructions on how mental illness is to be interpreted. This may seem to be a way to resolve the problem of psychiatric testimony, but, in fact, it simply rearranges the problem. It presumes that there are "psychiatric instructions," and neutral explanations of psychiatric theories and that psychiatrists as a group could agree on what they might be. Again, there is no way to corner psychiatric "truth," because it doesn't exist.

These solutions point toward the psychiatrist or psychologist, but he is not the problem—he is the scapegoat. Our need for psychiatric expertise is the product of our confusion and ambivalence about punishing others who seem like us in some ways and unlike us in others, and about punishing those who capture our sympathy and for whom we feel empathy.

It will not suffice simply to tinker with the system by eliminating psychiatric experts. We use them now to get us off the hook, but what will we do when they are gone? We will be alone on that hook and our human propensity will doubtless be to get ourselves off in some other, equally deceptive and perhaps worse, way. It is only by first facing up to the problem and to our limitations in solving the problem that any action can prove useful or helpful. Any solution must of necessity eliminate the hope of finding some way to assess mental states accurately. We must, at least as long as our knowledge is limited, give up on that as one of the elements of our resolution.

This is a great loss for us because we do have a very strong feeling that people who are mentally ill should be treated differently because they are different from us. Perhaps the only way to prevent abuses of our compassion is to treat all people as normal as far as the guilt phase of the trial is concerned and to let our compassion show itself in the allocation of punishment, rehabilitation, and treatment.

A workable solution would require the elimination of the insanity plea; the elimination of any testimony by psychiatrists about the actual or theoretical state of the defendant's mind at the time of the crime; the elimination of psychiatric expert witnesses in the guilt phase of a trial; and the requirement of a bifurcated trial that would, in its first phase establish guilt or innocence of the commission of the crime with no concern for the individual's state of mind in terms of mental illness at the time the crime was committed. The second phase of the trial, if guilt were found, would address itself to the appropriate disposition of the defendant.

In this second stage, if mental illness were asserted, the defendant himself would be obliged to testify. Jurors could thereby be given an opportunity to judge his mental state for themselves. Adversarial psychiatric testimony would be permitted, but it would be limited to clinical assessments, and would not include predictions or postdictions of behavior. This second phase of the trial would also require assessments of treatability, particularly testimony from those state institutional psychiatrists who, if the defendant were sent to them, would be responsible for providing treatment. Furthermore, these physicians should be prepared to specify at least minimum duration of treatment.

This system attempts to break down the idea that the defendant is either sane or insane. For example, defendants found mentally ill but amenable to treatment that would require a relatively short period of time would be given sentences that clearly included both treatment and prison. We can assume that a condition that is easily treated is only a contributory factor to the commission of the crime. For that portion of the defendant's actions, treatment is appropriate. For the remaining portion, punishment is appropriate.

This system provides a kind of sliding scale so that the less sane would receive more treatment, while the more sane someone is, the more punishment he would receive. It would provide treatment or punishment exclusively in extreme cases and some of each in the middle. Where we do not know what to do, custody would be provided. At the very least, it allows us to hedge our bets on what will work best for us and for the defendant.

What would be the effect of such an alternative on the cases in this book?

Dan White would probably have been found guilty of first-degree murder and received some treatment and much imprisonment. Since the average prison term served for first-degree murder in California is now thirteen years, he would have probably served at least that amount of time in treatment and prison. Under his voluntary manslaughter sentence, the maximum time White will serve is seven years and eight months, and he will almost certainly be released sooner.

Leonard Smith would probably have been found guilty of second-degree murder. He also would have received treatment, and then would have served approximately four to six years of prison time. Instead, he was given three months of psychiatric evaluation, four months of treatment, and then released.

Robert Torsney, if state hospital psychiatrists had testified that he was in no need of treatment, would have been found guilty of second-degree murder or involuntary manslaughter and served straight prison time for that offense. Instead, he was evaluated for ninety days and released after some months of legal argument.

Prosenjit Poddar was found guilty of second-degree murder before the California Supreme Court reversed the conviction. Under our revised system he would probably have been found guilty of first-degree murder and received substantial time in treatment and prison, and the California Supreme Court might have been less inclined to reverse his conviction on technical grounds.

Tex Watson would have probably been found guilty of first-degree murder (as he was), then found mentally ill, in need of treatment, and untreatable with any expectation of success. A first-degree murder conviction would have been appropriate, but if he were to regain control over his life—i.e., if time and prison itself acted as treatment—it is hard to know what would have been done with him. If psychiatrists did not consider him dangerous, then prison officials could decide whether the ordinary parole system might be appropriate for him. It is difficult to imagine that the public would ever again trust one who has so grievously abused his freedom. The prison officials, sensitive to public opinion, might well conclude that a Tex Watson, even if he seemed all right, is the exceptional case that may have to be sacrificed in order to make some sense of the handling of the vast majority of cases in the middle.

Under the revised system, Jim Grigson could not have testified at the trial of Benjamin Smith except to give the results of the mental status examination. He would not have been permitted to predict future dangerousness. The jury would have had to decide on its own whether Smith had shown himself so cold-hearted as to deserve execution. Hinckley would (among other things) have been found guilty of attempting to assassinate the president, but would also have been found mentally ill. He would have served prison time and received psychiatric treatment.

By requiring testimony from those mental health professionals who would be obliged to provide treatment on the probability of benefits or successful treatment, we bypass the problems of the Torsney-type case. Presumably juries' sympathies toward defendants would be greatly reduced if they thought that little or no treatment was needed or possible.

The case of Leonard Smith would presumably also be affected by such a requirement since the jurors believed, according to one of the attorneys in the case, that Smith, despite the not guilty verdict, would spend a substantial period of time in enforced hospitalization and treatment as a result of the insanity finding. That he would be treated and released within seven months was surely not part of what the jury envisioned as the result of their verdict. Smith did not testify in the second trial, which also suggests that the jurors had no way of judging for themselves whether his state of mind was abnormal at that time.

The idea that the punishment phase of the trial be split off from the guilt phase is not an unusual one. It is already the standard practice in many states today, for different purposes but for many of the same reasons. Guilt and punishment decisions are separated so that jurors' views on the death penalty will not affect their verdict about what crime was committed and whether the defendant was the perpetrator. Similarly, we urge the separation so that the concerns about whether the defendant should be punished or treated—postguilt decision issues—will not bias the jury's decisions about what crime was committed and what the defendant intended.

The guilty but mentally ill plea is appropriate only when the defendant has admitted the commission of the act in question. On the other hand, how the act should be defined may be a question for the judge or jury, that is, whether it is characterized as an act that the defendant contemplated (in whatever state of mind), planned (this would be comparable to first-degree murder), or whether it was a spur of the moment action (comparable to second-degree murder). Thus, for example, White's crime seems contemplated, as do Hinckley's, Poddar's, and Watson's; Torsney and Smith, on the other hand, seem to have acted on the spur of the moment. But it would require a judge or jury to make that judgment. It would not require psychiatrists.

Would such a system eliminate the actions of psychiatrists like Jim Grigson? Their testimony would be limited to clinical observations. They would not be allowed to make predictions and they would only be permitted to testify if the defendants were asserting mental illness as a factor in judging disposition. The American Psychiatric Association's opposition to psychiatrists' offering long-term predictions about dangerousness in criminal trials should be taken seriously. Although many people in and out of the psychiatric field argue that a short-term prediction of dangerousness is easy and reliable (both for the professional and the nonprofessional), there is no evidence that psychiatrists have any particular skill in predicting long-term dangerousness. Many in the profession think they can do it—Grigson included—but research studies have not borne out their contention. Parole boards do, in fact, have to make such judgments, but that is a different kind of system and process than the expert witness appearance in the criminal jury trial. Because parole boards must engage in such predictive behavior does not justify psychiatrists offering it for jury deliberation.

Many will complain that the elimination of the not guilty

by reason of insanity plea is a symbolic blow to our moral stature as a society willing to extend understanding and compassion toward our less fortunate members. But the plea seldom benefits the genuinely crazy. The psychotic, delusional killer Mark David Chapman, who shot and killed John Lennon, did not enter a plea of not guilty by reason of insanity. He had a vision in his jail cell that God wanted him to plead guilty and so he did. Was he crazy? Probably yes, before, during, and after the murder. In his case, there were no complaints about a lack of compassion or about how the criminal justice system permitted a crazy person to plead guilty. There was no outcry because no one wants to take chances with crazy killers. A genuinely crazy person—one with extremely deviant behavior but still competent enough to be tried—frightens jurors; if they feel that he is a potential danger to them (not personally a danger, but a potential, impersonal danger), then they will find him guilty. They are unlikely to find him not guilty by reason of insanity. Whether it is Charles Manson, Squeaky Fromm, or Mark Chapman, we do not want them free, and prison, rather than a hospital, is a more likely place for achieving that end. For all the talk about rehabilitation, the function of the prison is primarily to hold; the goal of the hospital is to cure and release. Jurors know that intuitively, and proven-dangerous crazy persons as well as proven-dangerous sane people go to prisons, not hospitals, so that they will not be released.

We must also keep in mind that, as Chicago columnist Bob Greene wrote, "Murderers aren't punished because they are unworthy in the abstract but because, on a specific date at a specific time, they crossed the line and killed." Compassion without standards of judgment is inappropriate and unwise as a public policy. It may suffice for individuals in their private lives if they choose such a path, but it will not do for a social rule.

Those who benefit from the not guilty by reason of insanity plea are the marginal individuals, not quite in control and not quite within the major range of normal behavior, but who are also not quite at the extreme. It is this group in the middle—not those at the end—that we must be concerned about. We do not probably treat those at the far extreme particularly humanely, but that is in part because we do not have any idea what to do for them. Lacking the ability to help them, we dispose of them in the prison equivalent of the locked, back wards of mental hospitals. Since we cannot help them, at least we help ourselves.

But in doing that, we have accepted an unfortunately rigid and dichotomous analysis of human behavior—sane and insane. The truly insane we throw away. Then we take what remains, and declare again that part of it is sane, part of it insane. But if a proper description of human behavior is a continuum rather than a binary model, we must come to terms with how to deal with the in-between group—those who are neither truly sane nor truly insane. It was obviously this kind of concern that created the original impetus for a defense like diminished capacity, in order to accommodate that behavior past the middle but not yet at the end of the continuum. Unfortunately, these solutions have not worked. Psychiatrists have lent confusion to the proceedings by introducing "information" that is based on strongly held but often arbitrary (or at least unproved and unprovable) assumptions about behavior and its causes. Juries have succumbed easily to this expertise. Whatever psychiatry has to offer to the legal system, it can best offer in the arena of clinical observations, assessments of treatability, and provision of treatment. Psychiatrists are not mind readers. They have no operative crystal balls that give them special views of the future or of the past. At their best, they are compassionate and highly educated professionals who can help some people to understand and change their behavior, and who can help others to find medication that reduces some of the disabling aspects of mental illness.

The legal system—judges, lawyers, and juries—must accept the responsibility for making decisions. It is neither fair nor honest to place the burden and the blame on psychiatry. Yet it is not even law that must face up to the need for harder decisions and more precise answers. The law and the legal system are only a collective mask for society. It is we who have tried to avoid answering these questions. If we accept reform in this area we, the jurors, will be obliged to stumble forth and assess guilt and punishment without the aid of medicine or science. It will be harder if we cannot share the burden of responsibility for our decisions, but it will be fairer, more honest, and less obscure. The guilty will be found guilty; the treatable will receive treatment; and the culpable will endure punishment. Some will be lost.